"Nick Spencer sensitively draws out the complex questions posed by agnostics, and New Testament scholar Michael Green addresses them with lucidity, charity, and understanding—getting to both the heart and mind of the honest seeker."

Ravi Zacharias, author and speaker

"Over the years books dealing with objections to the gospel or the serious questions of seekers have tended to stereotype inquirers and to prescribe responses that sound canned, impersonal, and even a little arrogant. Thanks to Michael Green and Nick Spencer for this splendid little compendium. 'I'd Like to Believe, But . . .' listens and responds to real people with a depth of understanding and a warmth of compassion that makes the gospel real to people by deed as well as word. Here are thoughtful, honest answers to real people, provided with the kind of winsomeness, sincerity, and love that we can only hope will rub off on everyone who reads this book."

Charles W. Colson, founder and chairman,
Prison Fellowship

"Michael Green has done it again. A book that is contemporary, relevant, and credible. In response to insightful questions about faith, he and Nick Spencer have given us profound answers that are so easy to understand."

Josh McDowell, author and speaker

"I have been a big fan of Michael Green for some time, and he has done an excellent job with his new work, 'I'd Like to Believe, But . . .' It should be a staple for anyone who wants to effectively share their faith with someone who has questions or skepticism. From the streets of London to San Francisco, this book captures the mind-set of our current culture that demands answers for questions of faith. I commend his practical writing style and illustrations throughout the book."

Scott Dawson, evangelist and author

"Michael Green gives a clear and straightforward discussion of some of the major concerns people have about the Christian faith. The strength of the book is that it is based on real questions from real people in the real world. I would recommend this to anyone investigating what Christianity is all about. It's brilliant stuff."

Andy Hawthorne, director, Message Trust

"Michael Green pulls no punches as he answers the voices of modern unbelief with love, humor, and the power of Scripture-based scholarship. Authentic on both sides, the contrast makes compelling reading."

Jonathan Aitken, author, broadcaster, and
former British cabinet minister

"I'd Like to Believe, But . . ."

Answers for Spiritual Seekers

Michael Green
and Nick Spencer

BakerBooks
Grand Rapids, Michigan

© 2006 by Michael Green and Nick Spencer

Published by Baker Books
a division of Baker Publishing Group
P.O. Box 6287, Grand Rapids, MI 49516-6287
www.bakerbooks.com

Printed in the United States of America

Library of Congress Cataloging-in-Publication Data
Green, Michael, 1930–
    I'd like to believe, but— : answers for spiritual seekers / Michael Green and
Nick Spencer.
        p.   cm.
    Includes bibliographical references and index.
    ISBN 10: 0-8010-6603-4 (pbk. : alk. paper)
    ISBN 978-0-8010-6603-0 (pbk. : alk. paper)
    1. Apologetics. I. Spencer, Nick, 1973- II. Title.
BT1103.G74 2006
239—dc22   2005030362

The particulars of the British edition of this work are as follows: Michael Green and Nick Spencer, I'd like to believe, but . . . (Leicester, England: Inter-Varsity Press UK, 2005). Copyright © Michael Green 2005. Inter-Varsity Press UK is the publishing division of the Universities and Colleges Christian Fellowship (a registered charity).

Contents

Introduction

Beyond Belief?

I was fascinated when I saw the slender volume *Beyond Belief?* by Nick Spencer, published in 2003. The volume is the result of a research project Nick conducted to learn about people's current beliefs. The research was done in England, but it is relevant to much if not all of the Western world. I have not been able to leave it alone and knew I had to respond to it.

Beyond Belief? is extraordinarily illuminating. Nick works for a very forward-looking organization, the London Institute for Contemporary Christianity, which published the volume. He does not generalize about attitudes in our contemporary world. He will have nothing to do with the over-simplifications that are commonplace in popular discussions of postmodernism and its effect on religion. Here is a serious market researcher taking the trouble to interview and discover the views of agnostics, who actually represent the mainstream of our population.

Nick's research method is explained in the appendix. The main points for us to notice at this point are as follows: Those he interviewed are thoroughly representative of our society. They do not go to church. They are unsure about God for a variety of reasons. Still, some of them would call themselves Christians; others would not.

The different faces of unbelief have long intrigued me, and I was immediately attracted to the results of this survey. By their own definition, the respondents were agnostic, and it is very instructive to examine their objections to Christian belief. Some of these objections were substantial and far-reaching, but many were disappointingly weak and confused. It reminded me how far many are from having any real understanding of the Christian faith, but the climate of the day draws them into rejecting the faith that many of them have never examined. Here are some quotations, derived from Nick's research, that show the spiritual hunger most people have. The comments are similar, irrespective of age, gender, or location, and they show a longing to believe—if only belief could be credible!

"My head tells me there isn't a God, but my heart wants to believe in it."

"Well, I suppose you could go to science and dismiss God altogether, but I think there is some sort of supreme power that is shaping our world—but what, I don't know."

"I think people who say they are atheist have not thought about it. It is a massive statement to make. I think these days people find it difficult to relate to most religions not just Christianity."

"I'd like to believe that there is a greater being of some description, but I don't know that I do believe in him."

"I can't be clear about whether there is a God. I find that very difficult to be absolutely sure about, but I do feel there is some kind of existence after we die."

"Without having that higher plane or greater being, you'd never have hope. Hope would be pointless."

"Without hope what have you got? Nothing to look forward to. So, what is the point of life? A lot of people see it like that."

"I refuse to believe that you are born, you live, you die, and that's it."

"I always wanted to believe it, but I can't from an intellectual point of view."

"I would love to believe. That is my whole thing. I would love to believe, but however hard I try or don't try, I have never had any kind of sign to me personally."

In a word, what many of these respondents are saying is *"I'd like to believe, but . . ."* I have written this book to try to remove some of those "buts." For it is to address questions like these, so honest, so open, so spiritually hungry, that our Christian gospel exists. Real Christianity makes sense of our questions, our longings, and our doubts.

My heart goes out to the thousands of people who are struggling with issues like these, who feel there is no solid ground on which they can stand. I am confident that there is solid ground. I hope this will become clear in the chapters that follow, as we look at some of the difficulties people have in believing.

As Nick and I talked, we were convinced that this book should be a joint project. At the beginning of each chapter, Nick has fleshed out the comments he received in his research, giving some personal background of the respondents. Then I have attempted to respond to the difficulties that are raised. As Nick reviewed my responses, he made many helpful suggestions. We hope the result will give new insight to open-minded agnostics as well as to Christians who want to connect with them.

1

"You don't have to go to church to be spiritual"

Melanie is fifty, married, and lives in the suburbs with her husband and two children. She considers herself to be a spiritual person and is open to mystical experiences. She has tried yoga and various types of meditation over the years but doesn't practice them with any regularity today. She believes in the existence of ghosts, although she has never seen one herself. She reads her horoscope in the paper religiously.

A couple of years ago an intelligent and trusted friend of hers had an out-of-body experience and this bolstered Melanie's sense of the divine, although she clearly feels uncomfortable talking about "God." Instead, she prefers phrases such as "something else," "somewhere else," or "another plane" and likes to talk about "spiritual energy."

Melanie had a token Christian upbringing. Her parents were nominal Anglicans and she attended Sunday school for a few years before the family moved to a new town. Her knowledge of

Christianity is, by her own admission, a bit shaky, but she definitely sees herself as a Christian. She wrote "Christian" on her 2001 National Census form and puts "Church of England" down whenever she is filling in forms on behalf of her children.

That said, Melanie is pretty much indifferent to the church. She enjoys the Christmas service and even attended her local parish church semi-regularly a few years back when her children were involved with Scouts. She was never really committed, however, partly because her association was primarily through her children but mainly because she couldn't accept the "narrowness."

"I think people can be extremely spiritual and have not necessarily committed themselves," she says. The idea that spirituality is bigger than the church is one of her recurring themes. "You can talk, pray anytime, all the time, wherever; it doesn't matter."

When asked about how she and other people might relate to God (a concept with which, somewhat surprisingly, she is perfectly comfortable), she says, "I don't think you have to go to church to relate to him. If you believe in him, he is always there for you and looking over you."

She admits, when pressed, that it is possible to be spiritual in church but unlikely. "The established church is built on rites and rituals," she explains. "It has so much dogma that I think it could be tried in a court of justice and could be found guilty of killing off spirituality."

She has no objection to Christianity, as such, but does not see its need. It is far better, she thinks, to practice your faith quietly, personally, and unobtrusively. "You can pray in the garden," she says, "but you can't do the gardening in a church."

●●●●

I have a lot of sympathy with Melanie and the views she has expressed. Let me point out some of the areas where we agree.

First, I like the fresh and natural way in which she expresses her spirituality. For the past two centuries, ever since the eighteenth-century Enlightenment when people rejected God and enthroned reason in his place, human spirituality has been crushed. It has, of course, sometimes erupted, as in the Romantic poetry of Keats and Wordsworth. Many of us had to read Keats's *Ode to a Nightingale* or Wordsworth's *Daffodils* when we were at school and we were touched by their warmth and spirituality. But these men, and the Romantic movement they represented, were exceptions. The main thrust of European thought was dominated by science. Only what we can touch and measure is real. Emotions are unreliable and unimportant. Well, in an atmosphere like that, spirituality cannot flourish. It retires into the shell of our private feelings and does not dare to emerge into the marketplace of ideas.

All this has been changing fast in the last twenty-five years or so. A growing disenchantment with the emotionless, dehumanizing tendencies of a narrowly scientific approach has been more and more evident. What is more, people are worried because science, while giving us unprecedented benefits, has produced the nuclear bomb with the power to blow the world sky high. An equal disenchantment has emerged with the pressures of the workplace, which has no interest in people's feelings, only in their productivity. We have begun to get in touch with our feelings again, valuing them highly. After all, it's love, joy, laughter, wonder, the soaring spirit that are really important in life.

For these and other reasons there has been a revolution against the cold, gray world of Enlightenment physics, chemistry, and regimentation. These days we celebrate the spiritual side of our nature, which has been too long neglected. And we are right to do so!

Melanie's second important insight is her impression that the church knows little about this kind of spirituality. It is a fair criticism. After all, when did you last laugh in church? When did you see love flowing through the congregation? When were the worshipers lost in wonder, love, and praise of the God they were supposed to be celebrating? Isn't a church service always run from the front? And usually by some sort of professional? Don't the people have only a minimal part to play? They may not even get a word of welcome as they come in. In many churches a man wearing strange clothes and using antiquated language reads the prayers out of a book. The hymn tunes are dreary and quite out of touch with modern music. And in real life nobody speaks for a quarter of an hour without interruption. After the service ends, there is sometimes not even a cup of coffee. The congregation seems thankful to go home!

To be sure, this is a worst-case scenario, but there are many churches that are still rather like this, and this is the impression that lasts with so many people who were forced to go to church as children and escaped as soon as they could. I cannot quarrel with the impression that some churches are unspiritual, but there is sure to be a church near most of us that is full of joy, is growing, appeals to all types and all ages, and really nourishes the spirit. It might be worthwhile seeking out one of these. They are, I am glad to say, on the increase.

There are one or two points I would like to make about spirituality. The first is that spirituality is indeed bigger than the church, but that does not necessarily mean that every form of spirituality is right or healthy! For example, Melanie says she believes in ghosts, but there is no hard evidence for the existence of ghosts as there is for Jesus. She believes in horoscopes and reads hers daily. Horoscopes suggest that the stars determine our lives. Holding such a view is the very opposite of being spiritual and liberated. It means that we are in bondage to cold forces that we can do nothing to change. People in the ancient world who had no understanding of a living God tended to believe in one of two impersonal forces—luck or the stars. Everything in life was either a lottery or else predetermined. A great fourth-century thinker who later became a Christian, Augustine of Hippo, used to believe that the stars controlled everything—until he noticed that people born on the same day under the same star had totally different lives. Then he realized how foolish this notion was.

I mention these two topics because they illustrate how spirituality can lead us wildly astray. There has to be some boundary to authentic spirituality, and this is what the Christian gospel offers us. Not, as Melanie noted, "the rites and rituals that kill off spirituality" but the guidelines of the God who made us and who loves us. He is no insubstantial ghost but the God who came among us to show us what he is like. This is no cold determinism from the stars but the freedom of knowing and loving God and sharing our lives with him. The spiritual side of our nature finds fullest expression in a relationship with God. What's the point of relying on some created object when you can know the Creator? What's the point of trying to quench your thirst elsewhere when you can drink the cool, refreshing water of a real relationship with the God who made you?

I am reminded of some words in the Bible spoken by the prophet Jeremiah long ago:

> Be appalled, O heavens, at this,
>   be shocked, be utterly desolate,
>   says the LORD,
> for my people have committed two evils:
>   they have forsaken me,

15

the fountain of living water,
  and dug out cisterns for themselves,
cracked cisterns
  that can hold no water.

Jeremiah 2:12–13

Not quite how we would describe it, with all our modern conveniences, but the point is clear enough. We have turned our back on God. We prioritize our pleasures, our relationships, our finances—and find they do not satisfy. My experience, and that of millions, is that when we change direction, and start bringing God back into the picture, we can, as Melanie says, "talk, pray to him at any time." Indeed, we will find that he is always there for us, looking over us. True, you can't do the gardening in the church, but you can talk to God as you do the gardening. I often do!

2

"The church is just too inflexible"

Annette, in her early forties, has three children, four dogs, two rabbits, and she works in a beauty salon. She likes to work out but doesn't have as much chance to do it as she would like, since she has "a second job as a taxi service," shuttling her children to rugby, swimming, Brownies, and Scouts.

She has had very little experience in church—some halfhearted and rather uninspiring experiences during childhood and since then just the occasional Christmas service and christenings, funerals, and weddings (including her own).

Her big problem with the church is that there are too many requirements. She had to jump through various hoops to get married in church and subsequently didn't bother getting her children christened.

"It's the inflexibility of them," she says. "You know, even when you go and seek them out, and even if you only want a part of their lifestyle or a part of their beliefs, they are not willing. They want you to have the whole package. And not all of us need that in our lives. Some of us want to be able to dip in and dip out. They are not that flexible, I feel."

As far as Annette is concerned, it is all or nothing when it comes to religion, and she isn't interested in the all. She doesn't agree with everything that she thinks the church believes and, therefore, as far as she is concerned, she is out of the fold.

In any case, she feels quite strongly about what she considers to be the church's responsibility to society and its refusal to fulfill it. "The church should reflect what we want," she says at one point. "The church should not dictate to us that you can get married or you can't get married. We want to get married. We are consumers of the church."

She hasn't vowed never to set foot in a church again—she admits to liking Christmas services—but she has no intention of turning to the church for spiritual help. The inflexibility she thinks she has experienced does not fit in with her lifestyle or with her image of what the church should be.

●●●●

Since Annette is in her early forties, her childhood churchgoing days would have been some thirty years ago. In those days the church, particularly the liturgical church, could be fairly described as inflexible. There was one set service for morning, evening, and Holy Communion—and it was all out of a book written three hundred years earlier. So the language was beautiful but so antique that you would need a dictionary to understand it. The clergy wore robes, which seemed alien to most people. Divorce and remarriage were not allowed. Indeed, the church was pretty inflexible, and that is a legitimate turnoff.

These days things are quite different. Unfortunately many people don't go near church, because they have been so fed up with what they experienced as a child. But if they do go, they will find great variety. You see, society has changed enormously in the last thirty years. It is the age of consumerism, the age of choice. Some of the liveliest churches have recognized this fact. The church is not meant to be a building or a hierarchy or an institution, but what the New Testament calls the body of Christ, which means it is supposed to be something like the visible expression of Jesus. And when Jesus was on earth, he did not isolate himself in a building or stand on his dignity. He mixed naturally with people, speaking not in proper English but in the common language that was easily understood, telling vivid and memorable stories, healing people who were ill, and in short being such an attractive person that people went into voluntary unemployment for a few days just to hang out with him.

Well, the church in recent years has been trying to follow Jesus's example. In matters of dress, for example, many churches have jettisoned robes in favor of ordinary clothes. The music has changed drastically. A mass of modern songs expresses today's worship, alongside the best of the traditional hymns. Many churches find even the modern revised services too stick-in-the-mud and operate on a diet of worship, testimony, Scripture, teaching (often with visual aids and back projection), prayer, and an extensive time of fellowship over coffee and something to eat after the service. You don't have to be able to find a hymn in a hymnbook or the Scripture passage in a Bible. Everything appears by computer-generated projection. Sunday is not the only worship occasion. Often midweek evening gatherings are more convenient, as people find their lives so crowded that the weekends are the only chance for some down time with the family in a heavily pressurized workweek.

But that is only the tip of the iceberg. Churches now take all sorts of forms. Almost everyone has heard of the Alpha course (check out alphacourse.org for more information). Its meals, its openness to questions of any kind, its clear presentations, and its friendliness are highly attractive. So is the opportunity to experience God's reality on the retreat, which features in all the Alpha courses. It's not surprising that many of these groups gain so much from the ten weeks or so together that they do not want to split up when the course is over. Some of them develop into churches of their own. And the whole process is aided by the growth of what are known as cell churches.

Worldwide, these cell churches are the fastest-growing and most relational way to live out the Christian faith, which, by the way, is winning adherents more rapidly than at any time in history. They never tell you that in the media, do they? But it's true. Cell churches represent a "two-winged" approach to being the church, stressing both the small and the large expressions of Christian community (the cell and the celebration). People often come together for a large celebration full of life and joy on Sundays, but the cell or small group lies at the heart of the movement. Normally the cell is made up of a dozen or so members who meet in someone's home. With leaders who are ordinary people, not clergy, the welcome is expansive and draws everyone in.

There are four main functions in a small-group meeting—worship, a teaching from the Bible (or perhaps the application of what was taught in the celebration the previous Sunday), personal care, and an evangelistic orientation. Everyone is actively involved in the cell, and individuals receive personal care and prayer for their needs during a time of ministry. The members of the cell invite others to come and join them. As others come, they are amazed by the warmth, relevance, and life of the cell. When the cell expands to a certain size, it splits into two groups, and the process takes off again.

Some may feel cell churches sound a bit too intense, but there are lots of other models. I celebrated Christmas this year in a fish and chip shop that the local church had recently taken over. It had been redecorated and repainted, but the counter remained where people could lean and put food and drink. There were no seats—they had not got around to them yet.

Everyone in the small town had been personally invited to the Christmas celebration, and loads of them came—with their babies, their kids, their presents, and their dogs. It was a wonderful time of worship, joy, laughter, and food, and a lot more like the original Christmas than some lofty cathedral worship—though there is a place for that too.

The small town of Bracknell in Berkshire offers another model. Mark Meardon and three musical friends in their twenties took over a small youth service called Eternity. Adults had planned it, but Mark changed all that. In January 1995, with a budget of twenty pounds, he and his friends set out to establish a community where young people could help plan the service and could experience God's love for themselves. Before long Eternity had grown to 150, with a core of young people meeting midweek in small groups for Bible study, companionship, and prayer for their friends.

In 1997 they started Evoke, a drop-in café. It was a low-key place to chill out on a Friday evening, and a lot of young people frequented it, but a year or so later the numbers began to drop. The youth culture was moving away from the café to the dance floor. So they kept the principle that was behind Evoke—a relaxed place where Christians and nonbelievers could meet and chat—but they allowed Evoke to die and created Eclipse in its place, complete with dancing, live DJs, Playstation, and a nonalcoholic bar. Now 100 percent of the youth in the town have made some contact

21

with Eternity or Evoke, and a quarter of them have entered into an active relationship with a church. Nobody could call that stuffy and inflexible, could they?

Another café venue for a church is Rubik's Café in Bristol. Open twice a month on a Saturday night, it is a magnet for those living in the area. People who have never gone to church go there and are gradually being drawn into the faith. Their other venture is Rubik's Cube, held every Monday and designed to speak to the bar crowd through music, food and drink, and friendships. Not only is it drawing people to Christ, but it was recently rated in a national DJ magazine as being "on the cutting edge of the drum and bass scene."

There are quite a lot of modern expressions of the church like this around the country, and they are showing that the church can be effective without being inflexible. People like Annette who have responded negatively to the rigidity of the church in the past are finding the contemporary church to be the most exciting thing in their life.

Annette also expressed concern that if she could not buy into all the church's beliefs, she would be "out of the fold." But the church doesn't work like that. You don't have to believe anything before you start attending. These days most people find a satisfying faith through belonging to a lively Christian community that they began attending before they believed much at all. It is certainly not a matter of all or nothing. If that were true, there would not be room for any of us in the church!

Annette said that "the church should reflect what we want. . . . We are consumers of the church." Sounds good but it won't really work. We are indeed consumers in shops where we can pick and choose, but we do not think of ourselves as consumers in our family. Well, the church is the community of Jesus, his extended family, if you like. It tries to march to his drum and go his way—it is not there just to give us what we want but to liberate us from our self-centeredness and make us a bit more like our leader, Jesus. So a church is unlike the supermarket; when we attend a church, we are not consumers. Rather, we are called to be disciples, or "learners," and to get stuck into God's family, with its need for give and take. If we stay on the periphery, we will never discover the joy of authentic Christian spirituality for ourselves.

3

"Christians are such hypocrites"

George, who is now in his early sixties, retired from the Civil Service a few years ago but works part-time as a delivery driver to "earn some spare cash and get out of the house." He is married and has three children and seven grandchildren.

Neither he, his wife, nor his children are religious, and George is quite proud of this fact. He is quick to defend his moral credentials and is profoundly irritated at the suggestion that he is a less moral person for not being religious.

"I've got high morals, but I would never say I was religious," he says. "I feel as though I've got morals. You know I'd never do anything to hurt anybody, whereas sometimes if you meet some people who are very religious, they sort of shove it down your throat."

When George was growing up, his family was strictly religious, with both parents attending their local Anglican church twice on Sunday. Thus he was very familiar with the church family and was comfortable with the various vicars and curates who came to tea. Consequently he had a good idea of what was going on and, as he got older, became less and less impressed with the difference between what he saw and heard in church on a Sunday and what he knew was going on in the parish.

George is adamant, however, that he is a Christian, writing "Christian" on the various forms he is required to fill out (including the National Census). He justifies this by explaining that there are two kinds of Christians, those who live decent, moral lives and those who go to church and make a big fuss of it. This latter group are, he insists, hypocrites.

"It's a kind of paradox, saying they are Christian, you know. Superficially they do all the things that Christians should do, but the way they treat others and behave and respond to crises, that actually is not very Christian." He continues, "Christians like to think of themselves as Christian, but in my understanding of the word they are not."

Having worked hard all his life and done his utmost to treat people fairly without ever boasting about it, George feels very strongly about the hypocrisy of those who (he thinks) like to proclaim their morality.

"My choice is that the church doesn't come into it," he says. "I just live my life as I believe I should live it and make my decisions and hope they are good ones. I don't have to go around pretending that I am going to be holy as long as I'm good and basically look after my family."

• • • •

There seem to be a few misunderstandings here. The first misunderstanding is the belief that Christianity is the same as being moral. It isn't! If it were, we could just call it morality not Christianity. Some of the most moral people who have ever existed have not been Christians. Think of Socrates and Plato in the ancient world or many Buddhists or Muslims today who have a very high moral code. To be sure, Christians have high moral standards too. They try to derive them from Jesus, who lived a

26

perfect life. But Christians are not so foolish or narrow-minded as to suppose that only they do good things and live a kind, unselfish life. What's more, they try to be quick to recognize their failures. This is the reason repentance or apology to God figures so prominently in Christian worship.

A Christian is a "Christ's man or woman." That's what the word means. A Christian has a personal relationship with Jesus, which is the Christian's defining characteristic. And he or she tries hard not just to keep commonly accepted standards but to please Jesus Christ. We don't always succeed, as you have perceived.

The second misunderstanding is that there are two sorts of Christians. There are those who don't believe in Jesus and don't go to church but write "Christian" on their census form. Then there's the other lot who are religious. Can the same name be used for both groups?

The first Christians did not call themselves by that name. They called themselves "disciples," which means "learners." They knew they had not yet arrived. Having just begun with Jesus, they recognized that they were on a journey and had not reached their destination. It was other people who called them Christians. Why? Because they behaved like Jesus, they spoke of Jesus, they sacrificed for Jesus, and they loved Jesus. The New Testament could never countenance the idea that you could be a Christian without following Christ and being devoted to him.

As the centuries passed, Christianity became the main faith of Europe, and indeed much of the whole world. Few faiths have ever approached it in numbers. So people began to call countries Christian if they had a majority of Christians in them. It was a broad generalization. Obviously not everybody in any country is a devoted follower of Jesus Christ. But because Christians try to live loving, generous, and sacrificial lives, people didn't object to being called that. And now in Britain where the number of Christians has shrunk a lot, the idea that a Christian life and a good life have a lot in common leads people to say that they are Christians when what they are really claiming is that they live good lives. You know the saying "I'm as good a Christian as those who go to church!" which means, "I live as good a life as those who go to church."

George feels very strongly about church people who go around proclaiming their morality. (I wonder if there really are such people.) And he points out that he has always done his utmost to treat people fairly without boasting about it. He says, "I've got high morals. . . . I'd never do anything to hurt anybody. . . . I just live my life as I believe I should live it and make my decisions and hope they are good ones. . . . I'm good and basically look after my family." It interests me that George says he doesn't like Christians who proclaim their virtues, but he seems to be doing precisely the same thing. However, George's main objection is that Christians are hypocrites, saying that religious people who go to church and make a big fuss of it are hypocrites.

The word *hypocrite* is an old Greek word. It means "actor." So the charge is that Christians are actors. They don't mean what they say. They are not real. I am ashamed to say that this is sometimes true—there are appalling scandals, which from time to time hit the headlines. It would be a mistake to start out with the idea that everyone who goes to church is a committed Christian. You will find people in Christian churches for all sorts of reasons. Some of them are seeking meaning in life. Some of them are simply battered by what they have been through. Some of them are habitual churchgoers—they go to church as thoughtlessly as they put their clothes on in the morning. Some of them may not be real, like Judas among the disciples of Jesus. Unfortunately, the Judas strain has remained in the Christian church.

Jesus was very vocal against hypocrisy in his followers (see Matt. 6:2, 5, 16; Luke 12:1). When you find Christians who are hypocrites, they are going dead against the teaching of Jesus. But I think you will find that as an overall description of Christians the charge of hypocrisy simply will not wash, and I will show you why.

Think of the first followers of Jesus, whom we read of in the New Testament. Most of them were killed because they could not keep quiet about Jesus. The same thing happened to many of their successors once the Colosseum in Rome was built at the end of the first century. For instance, Bishop Ignatius was torn limb from limb by lions. The strain of martyrs remains throughout the history of the church and continues today. In fact there have never been so many people killed for their loyalty to Jesus as in the past hundred years.

Think of the missionary movement in the nineteenth century. Men gladly went out to Nigeria with the gospel in the early days when the expectation of life was less than a year. And there were always those ready to step into the dead men's shoes. Think of the liberation of slaves, the passionate self-giving for the dying that we see in a Mother Teresa and her Sisters of Mercy or for destitute children in people like Thomas Barnardo. Any suggestion of hypocrisy is ludicrous. These people were real, so real that they did not count their lives as precious to themselves but were prepared to give them up for the

29

cause of Christ. Think of the politicians, educators, artists, poets, and musicians who have been inspired by Jesus of Nazareth, have used their gifts in his service, and have remained loyal to him until their dying day. There have been many blemishes in the church's record, but there is no faith, no ideology that has had such a distinguished record of public service, social and moral advance, and self-sacrifice as the Christian faith. If you removed all the Christians from Britain's voluntary services they would completely collapse.

Certainly a few of our church people may be actors. This was probably much more true in the Victorian days, when it was fashionable to go to public worship. Undoubtedly some went because it was the thing to do, but they remained strangers to Jesus Christ and did not allow their churchgoing on Sunday to affect the way they behaved from Monday to Saturday. That is the shame of the church. We Christians acknowledge that this is sometimes the case. When the church has been truly committed to Jesus and has reflected his life and his love to a needy world, however, it has had great value. Like many of us, George used to go to church as a youngster and saw things there that turned him off and made him cynical about Christianity. That's understandable. But I encourage George to take a second look at what has been achieved by genuine Christians. Look at Jesus himself. The failures of Jesus's followers may be disappointing, but Jesus is never disappointing.

When people flattered Jesus and called him good, he questioned it: "Why do you call me good?" he asked. "No one is good but God alone" (Mark 10:18). As St. Paul put it a few years later: "There is no one who is righteous, not even one; . . . no one who seeks God" (Rom. 3:10–11).

"There is no distinction, since all have sinned and fall short of the glory of God" (vv. 22–23). This is true of everyone. And that is why we all need a rescuer, a savior, if we are ever to get through to God. Mercifully, God has provided one.

4

"Religious people are too intolerant"

For about five years I have looked for spiritual direction. My inquisitiveness and my search still goes on but I am not hell-bent on finding answers. I am just waiting." So says Helen, mother of two late-teenagers, part-time librarian, and self-confessed spiritual traveler.

Having put much of her life on hold while bringing up the children, Helen is using her newfound spare time to explore life to the full. She and her husband have started to holiday in new resorts, eat at new restaurants, and explore new avenues in life.

One of these "avenues" is spirituality. Helen isn't quite sure what that means, but she feels sure that there is more to life than materialism and consumerism. To date, her spiritual search has not provided her with any answers, but she says she is quite happy to be inquisitive and just wait.

Helen is interested in a number of spiritual paths, but she has no time for Christianity or any other organized religion. The church, she reckons, is obsessed with rules and regulations and dangerously intolerant.

"One thing I am absolutely sure about is that I could not and would not want to embrace the church," she says. "Its narrowness—I think it is very bigoted. I don't think the church is willing to look at very important gray areas in life. I don't think it is truly willing to look at the very painful areas like homosexuality."

When pressed, she is unable to think of examples of the church's narrow thinking other than that of homosexuality, but that does not change her point of view. Religion, Helen says, is about control, whereas spirituality is about freedom. Religion is narrow-minded, whereas spirituality is open. Above all, religion is intolerant, whereas spirituality is about tolerance.

Intolerance, as far as Helen is concerned, is the root of the world's problems, and religion (as opposed to spirituality) is at the root of most of this intolerance. "If religious groups could respect each other's individual opinion, that would be really good, you know," she says.

As far as she is concerned, religion and religious intolerance (she uses the terms almost synonymously) are at the heart of most of the world's trouble spots—Northern Ireland, Israel, Kashmir, New York on 9/11. She doesn't quite claim that a world without religion would be a world without trouble, but she does think that religion justifies far too much intolerant small-mindedness, which breeds wars, terrorism, and atrocities.

She does not necessarily think Christianity is any worse than any other religion—she has a few choice words for Islam!—but she admits to not knowing enough about other faiths to comment on them. Christianity, she says, is bad enough.

Her opinions have had little impact on her spiritual search—she remains keen on exploring the spiritual world—but they have had a profound impact on the way she is searching. If the avenue has a hint of organized or institutionalized religion about it, she is not interested.

●●●●

A great many modern people feel the way Helen does. They realize that there is more to life than materialism and consumerism. They know that life gets blighted when we simply live for ourselves, for money, and for what money can buy. And that is a vital discovery. I know someone who asked, "What will it profit them to gain the whole world and forfeit their life?" (Mark 8:36). We can't get far without money, but money is a root cause of all kinds of evil, and to live for it is a destructive delusion. It is fascinating how many rich people go on record about how unhappy they are!

I am delighted that Helen has turned her back on consumerism and embarked on the spiritual search. That is very up-to-date, but it leads people to a variety of destinations: channeling, crystals, cults, oriental religions, Tantric sex, and bike rides to watch the sun go down over the sea.

Now that Helen's kids are grown, she is savoring a new freedom, and this freedom is immensely important to her—and indeed to all of us. Her search for spirituality has led her to make some inquiries into organized religion, which she has found wanting, and who can blame her? The average church or synagogue is not the most exciting place. It does not shout to us about freedom!

The very word *organized* is something that sticks in the throat of those seeking true freedom. They do not want to be told when to worship, when to stand up and sit down, or when to kneel. Such organization is the very antithesis of freedom, and unfortunately it marks most religious groups. Of course, I'm sure most of us would admit that some organization is a necessary part of life. If there were no rules of the road, for example, driving a car would be haphazard and dangerous. We need some organization to run a home, an office, or a country properly. Most people have had some organization in their home while bringing up the kids—who usually, when they are teenagers, react against the "house rules." No, it is not so much organization that is the trouble. The problem comes when organization crowds out life and inhibits personal growth and discovery.

I am intrigued by what Helen said about the love of the search. It reminds me of a mantra that used to be chanted in the days of my youth: "To travel is better than to arrive." Actually, religious people said that. They too were impatient with the control their religious observance seemed to impose, and they reveled in the freedom of travel rather than in the arrogant certainty of those who think they have arrived. And yet we do want to arrive. We may be content to wait for something that will really satisfy our love of freedom, but surely we don't want to spend our one precious life being perpetually uncommitted. G. K. Chesterton once said, a little unkindly, of H. G. Wells, "He thinks that the opening of the mind is simply the opening of the mind; whereas I am incurably convinced that the object of opening the mind, as of opening the mouth, is to shut it again on something solid."

There's another thing I want to look at: tolerance. These days intolerance is the ultimate no-no; tolerance is the supreme virtue. And this is a comparatively recent development. The fact is that once the majority of virtues go down the tube, tolerance is the only one left. And it had better be, or you will get a very bumpy ride through life. But it is interesting that in the New Testament you never find tolerance put forward as a virtue. A lot of other virtues are stressed, like gentleness, goodness, courage, unselfishness, and so on. But at the top of the tree is love not tolerance. Tolerance has a negative implication—putting up with other people. Love is positive—putting ourselves out for others.

There's a world of difference between the two. And when you stop to think about it, an all-embracing tolerance is not so impressive. Are judges to tolerate gangsters? Should we let pedophiles out among schoolchildren in the name of tolerance? Are all fouls on the football field okay if you have a nice tolerant referee? The idea is ridiculous. It sounds good, but we frankly don't believe it, nor can we live with it. Societies, games, and religious organizations have norms of expected behavior, house rules if you like. And if you join that society or sport or religion, you are expected to abide by the rules.

Of course that does not mean that religious organizations should be intolerant and unloving toward one another. Sometimes this has been the case. Sparks used to fly between different Christian groups, but you don't find much of that these days. I have spent a lot of time among people of different faiths, and I have noticed in recent decades something very important. We have learned to respect one another even if we do not agree with one another. That really is vital. We inhabit a small planet and if the different religions and ideologies do not learn to live with mutual respect, the outlook is very bleak indeed. That is why extremists of any sort, particularly suicide bombers, are such a threat to world peace and stability. Jesus was full of courtesy and respect for all types of people—churchmen, prostitutes, peasants, Roman soldiers—though he did not always agree with them. His followers must be the same. When they aren't, they betray their Master. Jesus told his close followers not to moan about others who saw their discipleship in a somewhat different light (see Luke 9:49–50). Most of all, he forbade the use of violence, even when one of his followers drew a sword to try to save him from arrest (22:49–51). "Turn the other cheek" (Matt. 5:38–39) was his teaching—and his practice.

Helen's main point is a very important one, however. She seems to be convinced that when we follow an organized religion, it must mean control. In fact the word *religion* comes from the Latin, and it means "something that binds or ties." The idea seems to have originated with a pact, an agreement between Numa, the first king of Rome, and Jupiter, king of the gods. It was a sort of "You scratch my back, and I'll scratch yours" arrangement. Numa would ensure that the smell of sacrifices always rose up to delight Jupiter's nostrils. For his part, Jupiter would ensure that the Roman armies always carried the day. And most religions are like that. They depend on rules that benefit both parties. But real Christianity is not like that. That is why I rather dislike calling Christianity a religion. It is essentially a relationship of love between an incredibly generous God and his grateful followers. And it is not about control but about free will and generosity on both sides.

Think of Jesus for a moment. He was the most liberated person that ever lived. He refused to be bound by the rules of the Jewish religion. You would find him scandalizing religious people by healing someone on a Sabbath day (see Matt. 12:9–14). You would find him eating food that the Jews thought ceremonially unclean (15:1–20). He refused to tolerate the corruption that went on in temple commerce but threw the moneychangers out of the temple (21:12–13). He freely chose to go to Jerusalem knowing he was walking to his death (16:21). If you read the story of Jesus on trial before Pilate, it is very obvious who is the free man and who is the craven coward (27:11–26). There was never a man more free than Jesus of Nazareth, and his followers need to be like him. Often they are not, and that is a very black mark against the Christian community. It is all too easy to allow our liberty as followers of the Great Lover to degenerate into legalism. This can be seen in many churches, but not in all. My observation is that there is a large proportion, perhaps a majority of churches, where relationship, not coercion, is the order of the day.

These are the churches that are true to the nature of Jesus. After all, what does he offer people? He is Christ the Liberator, and he offers release from guilt through free forgiveness when we do not deserve it one little bit. He offers freedom from habits that have chained us for many years, because his Spirit comes to live inside us and break their power. He sets people free from the fears that riddle our society—fear of terrorism, fear of what others think, fear that our good looks will fade, fear that the job will fold up, fear of death. Simon Peter came to realize that Jesus liberates people from fear. "Cast all your anxiety on him," he advised, "because he cares for you" (1 Peter 5:7). Jesus sets people free from the loneliness that enslaves them. He promises that he will be with us always, and that nothing in all the world can separate us from his love (Matt. 28:20). And one thing more. Jesus sets people free from aimlessness. So many go through life without any overall aim, just to get through the day or survive the week or to get married, have kids, and retire with a pension that has not shrunk too much.

But once you get gripped with the truth that Jesus is alive, he is risen from the dead, he is with you always—you have something to live for! It gives a new zest and purpose to living. It is true spirituality not religious control. Jesus never forces his followers to do what he wants. He asks them, and they are free to say yes or no. A wise man long ago said "Love God and do what you want." It makes sense, actually, although it sounds risky, because if we do love him, we will want to please him. Seeking to please Jesus Christ lies at the heart of Christian freedom. It is the true lover's response.

5

"You can't trust the Bible"

Adam, who has been working in South London for nearly three years, is thinking of moving on. He is twenty-four, single, and "between girlfriends." He plays soccer for his local team but is consistently disappointed with their performance.

Adam has no religious faith at all, although his upbringing was "quite Christian." His parents attended church irregularly when he was young, and he and his younger brother were "dragged along," willingly at first but against their will when they were older. There were better things to be doing, like playing soccer, on a Sunday morning.

Fifteen or so years of reasonably regular church attendance has given him a rudimentary understanding of the Christian faith and in a group interview with half a dozen peers, he is often able to correct them and lead the discussion when it comes to factual issues.

His basic objection to Christianity is that it simply isn't true. He is agnostic about the existence of God but quite certain that what is written in the Bible, which he recognizes as the foundation stone of Christianity, is not reliable.

"The Bible contradicts itself," he says. "There are stories in the New Testament from Matthew, Mark, Luke, and John—that's four different people, and there are often four different stories as well." The reason for this, he explains, is that "the Gospels weren't written at the time of Jesus but several years afterward. They were written well after Jesus died, so this fact would lend itself to the belief that the stories were exaggerated."

In addition to this, as far as Adam is concerned, historical records dating from so long ago are by their very nature untrustworthy. "Back then there weren't such things as the media, so it [the historical accounts] wasn't as widespread, like people didn't know about it as much." The idea of information being passed by word of mouth is proof of unreliability as far as he is concerned.

Adam asserts that not only are the Gospels contradictory but individual stories do not hold water either. "If you pull the Bible to pieces," he continues, "it's full of contradictions. For example, Adam and Eve had two sons. How did the world grow from two sons?"

And he believes that the Bible contradicts itself morally as well as historically. "You go through the Bible," he says, "and all the commandments are broken. So it's like, okay, you've got to do the Ten Commandments, but literally every one is broken, isn't it? So that's a huge contradiction."

The result of all this is that Adam has no interest in religion or Christianity. What's more, he is quite contemptuous of Christians who do not exercise the same skepticism of the Bible that he does. "They read it and they don't question it. That's what I don't get, because, me, I would question it."

● ● ● ●

The reliability of the Bible is an important issue. I am glad that Adam has raised it. I am particularly glad to read his final complaint: "They read it and they don't question it. That's what I don't get, because, me, I would question it." Quite right. We should question it.

You see, the Bible claims to be the record of the most staggering story in the world—that there is a living God who cares for us so much that he has made himself known to us. This record came to us first through the limited understanding of the Old Testament characters and prophets, but the climax and core of this record is when Jesus was born into the world. He claimed to reveal to us what God is like. The whole New Testament—the second half of the Bible—is concerned with the coming, the teaching and healings, the death and resurrection of Jesus, together with his massive claims. Those who were his friends and followers gave considerable testimony to the truth about Jesus. A lot of their testimony is incidental, written in letters they sent to the earliest churches of believers. That actually makes it the more impressive—they were not trying to prove a point, but they were trying to draw others into the rich companionship with Jesus that they enjoyed. This is how one of them, a close friend of Jesus, ends his account: "Now Jesus did many other signs in the presence of his disciples, which are not written in this book. But these are written so that you may come to believe that Jesus is the Messiah, the Son of God, and that through believing you may have life in his name" (John 20:30–31).

John, who wrote this, had followed Jesus closely for three years. Orthodox Jew though he was, he had gradually become convinced that this Jesus was no mere man, that he embodied all that could be known of God in human flesh and blood. This was the most important discovery of his life. So he was passionate to share it with others, not only during the rest of his long life but long after he was dead, through the book that he wrote. In it he gives seven great signs that show Jesus was more than human. He brought God into our scene. Then there was the greatest sign of all, the cross and resurrection. John tells us all about this. He tells us of an agnostic like Thomas, falling down at the feet of the risen Jesus, convinced at last that he really was the conqueror of death. Then John writes the passage I have quoted. He wants everyone to examine critically the evidence he has given about who Jesus really is. He wants them to go farther, as he had done when he was convinced by the evidence, commit themselves to Jesus, and discover to their amazement a whole new dimension of life. That is why John wrote his Gospel. He had found treasure, and he was determined to share it as widely as he could. In the centuries that followed, it has led literally millions to belief in Jesus.

Through the years from then until now, people have risked exposing themselves to the evidence in John's book. They have read it with an open mind. They have tried to find alternative explanations for the marvelous acts and words contained in it, but they have mostly failed and come to the same conclusion as John the author, that Jesus really did these things, really did die for us, really did rise from the chill of the grave, and can be encountered by anyone who is humble enough to seek him.

Many times I have talked to atheists and suggested there is a way by which they can be virtually certain whether or not the Christian story is true. I say, "Why don't you read this Gospel with an open mind?" Usually they tell me that they did that as kids when bits of it were rammed down their throat in Sunday school. But I say, "No, I suggest you read it in a different way, perhaps at a sitting. Let the story sweep over you. See what you make of it. And as you do so, ask God to show you what truth there is in it."

"I can't pray," they say: "I am an atheist."

I reply, "Well, here's a prayer you can use however atheistic you are: 'God, I don't believe you exist, but I don't know everything. I might be wrong. So if you do exist, please show me what is true in this stuff and I will follow that truth wherever it leads, even if it is to becoming a Christian.'" Of course, if there is no God, that tentative prayer will mean nothing. But in reading the Gospel you will have experienced one of the most beautiful and influential books the world has ever seen. And that can't be bad. It's a great way to pass the time between girlfriends! But be careful. Almost everyone to whom I have suggested this approach has become convinced that Jesus is real and has become a follower of his. It's all about having an open mind and letting the original evidence impact you.

Adam is worried that there are four different accounts of Jesus in the New Testament, the four Gospels as we call them. They have an enormous amount in common, but on quite a lot of points they differ. Of course no four people talking about their friend will ever say precisely the same things about him. They will all want to emphasize certain things. The Gospels are portraits of Jesus from different angles, painted by different people. They are not word-for-word the same. I should be very suspicious if they were. So would you if the *Sun,* the *Times,* the *Guardian,* and the *Mirror* reported the same football match in exactly the same words. They all give their own interpretation of the game. But that enriches our understanding and does not diminish it. It is like that with the Gospels. They each have a different slant, but they all present us with the same figure, towering over the merely human, full of vitality, insight, truth, and love.

Adam has another objection. The stories in the Gospels were not written down at the time they occurred but years afterward, and that could have opened the door for exaggeration and error.

Well, in the days after Jesus rose from the grave at the first Easter and sent his followers out to spread the gospel throughout the known world, they were too busy preaching the Good News of forgiveness and new life both now and after death to sit down and write books. But before long they did, as some of the eyewitness generation began to die off. Nobody is quite sure when the Gospels were written (certainly within fifty years of the death of Jesus), but a lot of the sayings of Jesus seem to have been taken down in shorthand during his lifetime. There were several forms of shorthand in existence at that time. Moreover the stories would have been repeated time and again in a fairly fixed way as preachers told them. As a matter of fact, both in Jewish and early Christian circles written testimony was not valued nearly as highly as oral tradition. In due course, but within the lifetime of those who had been with Jesus, these stories were written down. If they had cheated and made up the stories, others certainly would have exposed their deception, and the young Christian movement would have been finished. But nobody could rebut the evidence they recorded, because it was true.

I don't think we need to spend time discussing the children of Adam and Eve. It may be that the story was not intended to be taken literally but rather as a graphic picture of our creation, our dependence on God, our failure, and the first hints of God's rescue. If it is to be taken literally, then there must have been more than two sons born to Adam and Eve and there would have to be marriages among the other children—not a good move now, but inevitable under those circumstances!

Before we dismiss Adam and Eve too readily, let me note that some of the experts on the human genome project are coming to the conclusion that the whole of humankind descended from one woman, whom the scientists now call Eve. If all the different races did originally spring from a single female—well, that's something to think about! Also we don't need to spend time on the fact that God gives commandments and human beings fail to keep them. The Bible does not airbrush the nastiness out of life. It is shockingly honest about the failures of the men and women in its pages. It is that very human failure that called forth the love of God to the extent that he came among us to deal with the situation through the cross.

There are five good reasons for regarding the Bible very highly: First, the Bible has been relentlessly attacked through the centuries, and in our own lifetime particularly ruthlessly in communist countries. Not only has it survived, but it continues to be the world's best seller.

Second, and much more important, the greatest person who ever lived, Jesus Christ, gave the Scripture his unreserved support. He regarded it as inspired by God (see, for example, John 5:37–40). He saw it as utterly authoritative (Matt. 5:17–18; Mark 12:24). Time and again we find him saying, "The scriptures must be fulfilled." When he says, "It is written," that is final.

The third important reason for taking Scripture very seriously indeed is the fact of its many prophecies, which were fulfilled centuries later in the life and death of Jesus. Let us take four of them by way of illustration. Look up the whole of Isaiah 53; Micah 5:2; Jeremiah 23:5–6; Psalm 16:8–11. In these passages you find predictions of a coming great ruler in Israel. We are told the place of his birth, the family from which he would come, his reception by the people, the fact and the details of his agonizing death and what it would achieve, the circumstances of his burial

47

and his ultimate triumph. These prophecies were precisely fulfilled in Jesus. There is no parallel to such fulfillment of prophecy anywhere in world literature. Isn't that very odd if the Bible is unreliable?

The fourth reason for giving great heed to Scripture is this. The Bible is not so much a book as a library. It was written during a period of fifteen hundred years, in three languages, by an incredible variety of people. But you find one single picture of God—utterly loving, utterly holy and just, and the personal creative source of all life. You find one single picture of human beings—neither "naked apes" nor "little angels" but made in God's image and yet constantly going our own way and leaving him out. All the chaos in human affairs springs from this basic attitude of rebellion. And you find one single picture of divine rescue. He cares for us so much that he welcomes us back into his company though it cost his death on the cross to make it possible. Now if you get ten people together in a room, you are likely to get ten different views of God, humans, and salvation. Is it not remarkable that this book, the Bible, has such a unified view on these vital issues? Does it not suggest that behind the very varied human authors here was the all-shaping mind of God, longing to disclose himself to us?

And that leads me to my final conviction that the Bible really is God's message to us: experience. Once you start reading it, seeking to live it out, you become increasingly convinced of its truth, its wisdom, and its power. Anyone who has not read it should give it a try!

6

"Science has disproved Christianity"

Keith is married, in his late forties and has two children. He works as an engineer and likes to think he has a clear, concise, rational mind. He is disdainful of the "hocus-pocus" of spirituality and pseudoscientific practices like alternative medicine. For him religion falls well within this category.

As far as Keith is concerned, the universe is an enormously complex but ultimately comprehensible and predictable machine, and the tool for understanding it is science. He illustrates this in a number of ways.

Generally speaking, science has proved itself much better at explaining the world than religion. "We know how the world began and, you know, science questions the creation theory and all these other things." And this explanatory success is evident in virtually every aspect of modern life. "With science you see a lot. You see the science that allows people to have babies through IVF and things like that."

More specifically, according to Keith, science has disproved a number of religious claims, creation being the most obvious one.

"Christians say that the world was made in six or seven days and on the sixth day humans were made, but where in that six days were the dinosaurs made and when did they get wiped out? It's like Darwin's theory of evolution and the discovery of bacteria at the bottom of the sea and all that kind of stuff, millions and trillions of years old. That makes a lot more tangible sense to me than this mythical God that is up there who is supposed to have single-handedly created the whole world, as is."

Another example of how science has supposedly disproved Christianity that he cites is the Turin shroud. "You've got the Turin shroud, haven't you? Scientists are now saying it couldn't possibly have been the robe that Jesus was buried with. So that is down to science again, isn't it?"

When pushed on these issues, particularly the issue of creation, which in his mind is the most substantive disproof of Christianity, his reasoning becomes slightly more hesitant. He acknowledges, for example, that the world does seem to be shot through with signs of design, although he insists it's an optical illusion, in the same way as the sun appears to circle the earth. More surprising, when another, even more skeptical person in the discussion group presses him for proof of evolution, Keith says, slightly sheepishly, "Even now you've got people who have got features that are more apelike than others, haven't you?"

He is also willing to recognize the comfort that believing in God may offer people, but he puts this down to wishful thinking. "I don't believe, because there's not enough scientific basis for it. It would be nice to believe that Santa exists too!"

● ● ● ●

Let's begin with Keith's main point about creation. There are not many Christians these days who believe that the world was made in six days—six twenty-four-hour periods. For example, the seventh day is clearly not a matter of twenty-four hours but represents God's Sabbath rest that still continues today. Neither Jewish rabbis nor early

Christian fathers like Origen and Augustine imagined the world to be created in seven periods of twenty-four hours each. There is a good reason for this, for frequently in the Bible the word *day* is used of a long, unspecified period of time. We must not dismiss the biblical account because of a misunderstanding.

Science has Christian origins. Modern science was born in the sixteenth and seventeenth centuries in a Christian civilization, recently liberated from the shackles of religious authoritarianism by the Renaissance and the Reformation. It was pioneered by Christian men who saw God's works in nature and his words in Scripture as the twin facets of his self-disclosure. Keith seems to think that the universe is an enormously complex machine. Few modern scientists would agree with him, but that was the view, broadly speaking, of Isaac Newton. He certainly did not see belief in God as incompatible with his model of the universe. He wrote his *Principia* in the assurance that "this world could originate from nothing but the perfectly free will of God." And Einstein, whose theory of relativity made a massive advance on Newton, was also a strong believer in God the Creator. Many of the founders of the Royal Society, scientists like Robert Boyle, Ward, and Isaac Barrow, saw no contradiction in directing their studies equally "to the glory of God" and "to the advantage of the human race."

But there is some truth in the idea that, even if science originated in Christian circles, a great divide has opened up between science and religion since Darwin's theory of evolution emerged. In the latter part of the nineteenth century, there was a growing desire among English scientists to free themselves from church influence. They were not opposed to Christianity as such but rather to the control exercised by the Church of England. Science needed to assert its independence. That is the real reason why the partnership between Christianity and science, which was strong in the early part of that century, collapsed. In the first half of the nineteenth century, a country parson like Gilbert White pursued his scientific studies in *The Natural History of Selbourne*, confident in his science and sure of his God. But later in that century the famous and ill-natured debate between Thomas Huxley and the Bishop of Oxford about Darwinian evolution was prominent. Their positions were irreconcilable—and both thought they had won the argument!

To be sure, lots of people share Keith's view that science has disproved Christianity. That's almost a basic assumption for the person in the street, and it is supported by that crusader for atheism Richard Dawkins, who is always drawing a contrast between "scientific proof" and the "blind faith" of believers. This is a contrast that looks impressive but simply will not stand critical examination (see Alister McGrath's book *The Twilight of Atheism*[1]). The person who believes there is no God is just as much a man or woman of faith as the person who believes in God. They just believe different things, which neither can conclusively prove! What we need to examine is not belief but evidence. Evidence is the only solid ground on which belief should rest.

Science does not prove things. Scientists observe, and when they see a series of uniformities, they suggest a general law to account for them. Then they look for evidence to support or to counter this "law" that they think they have found. But evidence is not absolute proof. It is capable of being reassessed and modified. For centuries it was regarded as self-evident, on universal observation, that all swans are white—until Captain Cook found black swans in Australia! One contrary instance can cause scientists to revise their theories so as to include both the observed uniformities and the exception. Scientists call it "radical theory change." They would be the first to admit that science has not proved everything, and that their theories do change. These days the best scientists have a proper humility before the complexity of the world. They look for evidence of a general law, but they are open to evidence that causes them to rethink theories. That is precisely the way Christians operate, by the way. They look at the evidence for God's existence (see chapter 12), they examine the life and teaching of Jesus of Nazareth (see chapter 8), and then they decide whether the evidence warrants belief in God and commitment to Christ. Self-commitment is based on evidence. Scientists call it "inference to the best explanation," but it is open to revision. Thoughtful Christians operate in just the same way.

The best scientific theories are not the narrowly detailed ones but those that look for the big picture and the explanation that makes most sense of it. When you put together the evidence, outlined in chapter 12, with the fact that we can make moral judgments, relate to one another, appreciate beauty, and think, you can appreciate why many people decide that the existence of God is the best explanation for the totality of our world and ourselves.

Let's pause on this thinking business for a moment. The fact that we can explain anything at all is remarkable and calls for an explanation. "God is revealed," said the astronomer Johannes Kepler, "both in the world and in the human mind reflecting on the world." In other words, there is a resonance between our minds and the way the world is. Is that compatibility between the mind and the external world an enormous fluke, or does it suggest that there is a living God who is both the source of our world and of the minds with which we seek to understand it? Books by the top scientist John Polkinghorne make much of this remarkable point.

The fact of the matter is that the natural sciences neither prove nor disprove the reality of God. God is not small enough to be caught in the analytic net of the scientist. There is not just one way of knowing. The scientist who measures his material in the test tube and knows what he is doing does not know his wife in the same way when he goes home. At least, he would be in deep trouble if he tried! There is a world of difference between what the philosophers call "knowing by description" (the scientific way) and "knowing by acquaintance" (the way we know friends—and God). But both are valid. Nor must we shrink God to cover the ever-decreasing gaps in our knowledge. The "God of the gaps" is a pathetic travesty of the dynamic, infinite, all-pervasive God of the Bible who is at the same time immanent within every aspect of his universe ("in him all things hold together," Col. 1:17) and also immeasurably transcends our every conception ("he . . . dwells in unapproachable light," 1 Tim. 6:16).

You have to look at the evidence and see whether the atheist or the theist hypothesis makes the most sense. But let's have none of this rubbish about science killing off Christianity. Did you know that some 40 percent of active top-level scientists are Christians? Certainly they don't believe that science has disproved Christianity. Moreover, the late American evolutionary biologist, Stephen J. Gould, an open-minded agnostic who was one of the world's leading

Darwinian scholars, wrote: "To say it for all my colleagues for the umpteenth million time: Science simply cannot by its legitimate methods adjudicate the issue of God's possible superintendence of nature." He continued, "Either half of my colleagues are enormously stupid, or the science of Darwinism is entirely compatible with religious belief and equally compatible with atheism."[2]

Interestingly enough, Charles Darwin contemplated ordination early on in his life and carried belief in God into his studies in evolution. But his views on God became increasingly confused as he grew older, and he seems to have ended in agnosticism. But it was not because his evolutionary studies led him to deny the existence of God. The problem lay much closer to his heart. He was deeply upset by the death of his daughter, his own father's agnosticism, and the consequences for his family in light of the church's doctrine of hell. Darwin understood well that science is neutral. While he seems to have moved toward agnosticism, his close associate and fervent evolutionist Asa Grey remained a deeply committed Christian. As Nietzsche put it in another context: "There are no facts, only interpretations!"

Once we are clear on this, other answers may fall into place. The earth may be, as Keith says, "millions and trillions of years old." Many Christians are totally open about its age. It makes not one iota of difference to our faith in an intelligent Force we call God what evolutionary or other processes brought the world to its present state. Keith's concern about the death of the dinosaurs is utterly irrelevant to the discussion. They were possibly, even probably, wiped out by the fouling of the atmosphere and the darkening of the sun after some massive meteor hit the earth, and I am very happy to accept whatever date you like to give for this. It makes no difference to Christian belief!

Range of perspectives . . .

As for the Turin shroud, the Roman Catholic Church deserves credit for the willingness to have it tested. This remarkable object had been a cause of controversy for many years, and in the interest of clearing up the matter, the church released a piece of the shroud for scientific analysis and accepted the result that it was very unlikely to have been the garment in which the body of Jesus was wrapped, since it apparently derived from the Middle Ages. That is hardly a battle between religion and science. Christians have no investment in believing that the shroud is genuine. Our faith in Christ is not altered one way or the other. And the church did the right thing to encourage proper investigation—and then accepted the result. Curiously enough, the issue of its genuineness is apparently not closed after all. In March 2004 there was a TV documentary showing that the most recent research suggests strongly that the shroud is very probably a first-century AD product from Palestine.

Keith's desire to explain as an optical illusion the design that can be recognized in nature seems far-fetched. How would that work for the radar of a bat or the spawning habits of a salmon, traveling hundreds of miles to the river where it was born to lay its eggs? How could the direction-finding mechanism of newly hatched young birds that migrate thousands of miles to a tiny island in the midst of the Pacific that they have never seen be written off as an optical illusion? And speaking of optics, where did the immensely intricate design in the focusing equipment of our eyes come from? Keith's description of this as an optical illusion doesn't make sense. And his pointing to some of his fellow men as having apelike faces is not only rude and probably racist, it fails to recognize the vast periods of time that need to elapse if evolutionary theory is true. We must be careful to examine the evidence closely and avoid making uninformed judgments.

7

"There's just too much suffering in the world"

Morris, at forty-one, is the father of one daughter, aged six. He is an open and positive individual with a particularly moving story.

"I got a huge amount of support from the church, because my wife was ill. She was quite Catholic, and she got a huge amount of support from the local Baptist church. She was ill for about two or three years, and when she died, my daughter and I, we got a lot of support from them. It was just what I needed from fellow human beings. It was a real community spirit, you know, inviting us to their houses, bringing food to my house. It was totally genuine. When it's from the heart, there's a difference. They didn't expect me to actually go to church, although I felt as though I should have gone and continued to go, but my beliefs had changed and I don't think they frowned on that, you know. I could have continued, I could have perhaps converted in some way, but I didn't."

In the group of which Morris is a member, his story begins an interesting conversation. Other respondents echo his sentiments, though they haven't had the same personal experience.

"Sometimes I think it would be nice if God did exist," one individual says, "but then I think about, like, there's some really terrible things that happen in the world and I think, if there was a God, why are all those horrible things happening?"

Some other interviewees refine this sentiment. "It can't all be good," one says. "No, it can't be. We have to see suffering." Another makes the point that human beings themselves are responsible for much of the suffering in the world.

"People dying hungry, that's probably because the governments aren't investing or the money is going elsewhere on arms. So a lot of these disasters that we have, you know, man makes himself."

Someone else points out that there is a certain hypocrisy in the way we blame God for bad things but don't thank him for good ones.

"You always seem to ask the question when things are going wrong for you—why me? But when things are going all right, you never seem to think, 'Oh, well, I'm the lucky one.'"

Slowly, a consensus on this most complex, painful, and personal of issues begins to appear in the group's discussion. God cannot be blamed for human wickedness, at least not directly, and suffering can, sometimes, bring about good. But, that said, God is responsible for natural disasters, except perhaps those that result from our abuse of the environment.

"If God created the world, why does he allow things like earthquakes and famines and droughts and natural disasters to happen? Not man-made disasters, I mean, things like wars man creates for himself, but natural disasters. Why does he allow them to happen?"

The concluding tone of the debate begun by Morris's story is one of resignation rather than anger. God could have done a better job in creating the world, but human beings are not entirely free from blame.

••••

Suffering is a fact of life. Whatever our beliefs, we all have to face it. Nobody has the luxury of being able to philosophize about it from an armchair. As part of our human condition, mental, physical, emotional, and relational pain and suffering will touch every one of us. How are we going to make any sense out of it? How are we going to handle it when it comes along? That is the real issue.

Morris has handled his suffering with great strength of character. He had not a word of complaint against God when his wife died but enormous appreciation for the support the local Baptist church gave him and his daughter—not just a meal or two after the funeral but continuing support and warm companionship. He realized that it was totally genuine. And when kindness like that comes from the heart, it makes an enormous difference. It nearly made him join them in that church—but not quite. That particular church gave an example of true Christian caring, without any strings attached, for a fellow human being going through a personal tragedy.

Morris's experience and willingness to talk about it with the interview group clearly stimulated their discussion. Some were in agreement. Some were wistful, thinking how nice it would be if there were a God, but the problem of suffering seemed to preclude that possibility. Some were honest enough to admit that we blame God when things go wrong but don't come back and thank him when things go well. But the really interesting and unusual turn in the conversation came when some of the group got around to admitting that a great deal of the suffering in the world is man-made.

They really put their finger on it. The major cause of human suffering is the misuse of human freedom. One of the most precious attributes we have is our freedom. God cannot and will not take away our freedom when we use it against him. He will not intervene to stop train accidents when someone has forgotten to change the points or to stop the plane being blown up when airport security has allowed a suicide bomber on board. The people in the group realized that hunger in the world is due not to the lack of food (there is plenty of food for everybody if only it were fairly distributed) but to selfishness, corruption, and inefficiency in governments and protectionism by rich states. At present there are more than thirty thousand children who die every day from preventable diseases because the rich countries simply do not care enough to help. The same applies to wars, marriage breakdowns, and many other forms of human suffering. It cannot be laid at God's door. Human beings are responsible.

Another important point that the discussion surfaced was that suffering can sometimes produce good. Although God does not send suffering, he can and does use it. The pain and irritation in the oyster is what produces pearls. In human character, qualities like courage, self-sacrifice, and endurance can come about only in the face of suffering. Sometimes in my work I have found people changing into integrated, joyful Christians after a death or some other disaster in the family. Sometimes the experience of acute suffering makes people intensely sensitive and compassionate toward others in need. Sometimes the way a person handles suffering lights up a whole hospital ward. I recall a Christian with the wasting disease who had a phenomenal influence on the whole hospital ward and nursing staff. Supremely, of course, the cross of Jesus Christ shows how much good can come out of suffering and apparent disaster. His death has proved the inspiration for millions of innocent sufferers, and through his death, he took responsibility for the guilt of all who would turn to him.

The most difficult type of suffering for a Christian to explain is that caused by natural disasters like earthquakes and famines. We believe both that God is good and that God is loving, so how can such things be allowed in God's world? With other faiths the problem is not nearly so acute. Christianity is not like Buddhism, which sees suffering, in the final analysis, as an illusion. The Bible sees it as agonizingly real. Christianity is not like Hinduism, which sees suffering as an inevitable principle of retribution, the outworking of karma. You sin; you pay for it through suffering. Christianity is not like Islam, which relapses into fatalism in the face of suffering. "It is the will of Allah." No, the Bible teaches that God does not willingly afflict us. Christianity is not like modern Judaism, seeing suffering as atonement for sins. Christians realize that no man-made atonement can make us guilty human beings right with a holy God. Nor is Christianity like atheism, accepting suffering as an inexplicable fact in a godless universe, which we simply have to put up with, because we have no choice.

For Christians the whole problem is more difficult. We believe in a Creator God who is both powerful and loving. Why then do we have famines and earthquakes?

I think we have to begin with the link that the Bible makes between the fault line that runs through nature and the fault line that runs through human beings. They are linked, not only in the creation story but in our experience. Belatedly we are coming to realize that this world is so precisely ordered that even a small disturbance in one part of it can affect areas that are thousands of miles away. Think of the so-called butterfly effect by which a large hatch of butterflies in Latin America can produce flooding in the

Indian Ocean. Or think of the way the destruction of the rainforests is having the most devastating effect on the world's climate. Think of the way emissions from our cars and refrigerators are piercing great holes in the protective ozone layer. Or think of Libya and Tunisia, once the great wheat fields of the Roman Empire, now irretrievable desert. The link between the damage to our environment and human mismanagement and greed is very evident.

Earthquakes generally take place along well-known fault lines in the Earth's surface, where underlying plates overlap. Recently I saw a map showing where the earthquake hot spots were in the days of the dinosaurs, and superimposed on it was a map of where they occur now. They are in almost the identical places. Human beings have long known the dangers of living and building along such fault lines but have continued to do it. Vancouver, where I worked for some years, is on the San Antonio fault line and is sure to get a massive earthquake one day. If so, it would destroy the international airport, built only a few feet above sea level on a little island. But does that thought stop people building there? Not at all. And yet they will be sure to blame God when the earthquake comes! What's more, most of the devastation in earthquakes happens when poor materials or shoddy craftsmanship are used in constructing houses—and that is a human failing. The buildings built to earthquake-proof specifications almost always withstand the quake.

Well, you may say, couldn't God have done a better job of creating the world? Two answers immediately come to mind. First, since the days of the first-century-BC Roman writer Lucretius, people have dreamed up improvements on world design, but they have all been shown to be utterly unworkable. Any change would make things worse not

64

better, so carefully balanced is our universe. And second, if we want a Christian explanation of suffering, we must go to the Bible.

The Bible makes it plain that the world as we know it is not as God originally made it, for human wickedness has affected the fabric of the created order. Nor is the world as it will one day be. It is a world in the making. God is ceaselessly working for the renewal and transformation of the world and has plans for its complete renewal. This is demonstrated by the bodily resurrection of Jesus, where the stuff of his physical makeup, cruelly put to death, was raised with its constituent elements transformed so that it had new and more wonderful properties. It may help to see it as the change from gasoline to energy. It has the same elements but different form. One day the "new heaven and the new earth" that God plans will be like that. At present we must not complain if the created order does not manifest the utter perfection of God, its Creator. And it may be that earthquakes, part of the seeming disorder in the world, may actually be part of extremely complex solutions, to which we may at present be blind. After all, nonequilibrium is the source of balance!

But we must not miss the heart of the Christian teaching about God and suffering by concentrating too much on interesting but marginal parts of the problem of suffering, like earthquakes. The utterly unique thing that Christianity reveals to the world is a suffering God, a God who understands our pain and frustration because he has willingly entered into it himself and drained its anguish in the most excruciating death it is possible to devise, crucifixion. God may not have given us a perfect intellectual understanding of the mystery of suffering, but he has given us an awesome insight through the cross of Jesus into the sort of God he is. He is no blind despot pulling the wings off flies. He is not so far removed from the world that he does not care about our agonies. He is the God who came down onto the factory floor of the world and got his hands dirty. He suffered as we suffer, only more. On that cross the center of his suffering was not the physical agony but the anguish of carrying the load of the world's guilt, guilt that not only had separated us from God but had affected the very fabric of the world we live in. And by that marvelous combination of Good Friday and Easter, he showed that sin and suffering would not have the last word in God's world. Tragedy will give way to triumph. It did for Jesus and it will for his people, not necessarily in this life but after this life, for you can never get a proper handle on the problem of suffering if you restrict yourself to this life alone. This life, as Keats put it, is "a vale of soul making," and it is in the life to come that we will be able to look back and say it was worth it. And Jesus will be able to say, "Yes, I know. I have been through it too." By far the wisest thing, then, for puzzled and suffering human beings to do is to bring their pain to the wounded hands and broken heart of the God-man who loved us and gave himself for us.

8

"All the religions in the world can't be true"

· ·

Karen works at a gas station in south London. She was born and educated in a thoroughly multicultural community and has several Asian friends as well as a Hindu and a Muslim colleague. She doesn't know much about their belief systems but has been aware of their different cultures for as long as she can remember. She admits to sometimes feeling resentful about what she views as her culture—English, white, Christian—being superseded by others that are less familiar, but she vigorously denounces racism.

Her grasp of interfaith issues is slight but her lifelong awareness of multiculturalism has convinced her that since not all religious claims can be true, none of them is. She is uncertain of this conclusion, however, and often brings it up in conversations. "If there's only one God, why the hundreds of religions?" is her opening gambit. "As you begin to appreciate all of the faiths you understand that they've each got their own God. That's very hard to reconcile."

When gently pressed on these ideas, she changes tack: "Even though there are hundreds of religions, they do sometimes believe in the same thing, for example, that there is someone higher up looking after them. The differences are because they've got different influences from different parts of the world." Thus she seems to think that all religions are essentially the same, though shaped by the various cultural influences inherent in their origins and development. She admits to not knowing enough about the particular beliefs to help her answer these questions.

On final consideration, however, she changes tack again and refers to what she does feel confident she knows about religions to reach a (tentative) conclusion. "Some of them believe that there are several gods and some that there is only one. Some religions say that their god made the earth and then Christianity says their God made the earth. And, you know, someone's got to be lying."

●●●●

I love the way Karen makes her points about the great variety of faiths and cultures. She displays an engaging modesty in her approach to this complicated issue. She is not embarrassed to backtrack and change her mind at times, though her main point is very clear: They can't all be right!

I'll come to that in a minute. I want to comment on the fact that Karen works among colleagues of different faiths, and they get along pretty well together. The same thing often (but not always) happens on the broader stage of world affairs. We live on rather a small planet, and unless we learn to get along with one another, there is precious little hope of survival, with all the sophisticated weapons of mass destruction we have invented.

Recently I attended a remarkable meeting in HM Treasury. It was a day working on a plan to bring new hope to the poorest of the world's poor. The president of the World

Bank, the Chancellor of the Exchequer, the economist Lord Griffiths, and the heads of big business, relief organizations like Oxfam and Tear Fund, along with musicians like Bono and Bob Geldof were all there. They were united in determining to work to improve the state of the world's poor by raising an additional fifty billion dollars a year. Religious people were there as well, including the newly retired Archbishop of Canterbury, the Chief Rabbi, Cardinal Murphy O'Connor, the head of the Muslim Council of Great Britain, the president of the National Council of Hindu Temples, the head of the Sikh Council for interfaith relations, and many others. These leaders of the world's great faiths were united in a determination to do the right thing together, to eradicate extreme poverty, to create justice in trading, to remit crippling debt that can never be repaid, and so forth. It's good to see that the many faiths can unite for a noble purpose.

Having said that, as Karen points out, they can't all be right in their beliefs. So a bit of clear thinking is in order.

First, it will not do to suppose it does not matter what you believe as long as you are sincere. I may sincerely believe that all roads from Oxford lead to London or that a little cyanide on my soup is good for me—but I would be wrong!

Second, it will not do to suppose that the religions are all basically saying the same thing. They don't even all believe in someone up there looking after them. Buddhism, for example, does not believe in God at all. The Allah of Islam is very far away and you can never know him. In Satanism the ultimate force is evil not benevolent. In Hinduism there are many gods but behind them all there is one impersonal unity, which certainly does not look after us. The sheer variety of beliefs makes them completely irreconcilable.

Third, it will not do to suppose that all the religions are different roads going up the same hill and all will meet at the top. Buddhism believes you can save yourself by your noble deeds. Christianity believes your good deeds are never strong enough for that job. God alone has done all that is necessary to put us right with him. Hinduism believes that the principle of karma operates everywhere. It means "you sin, you pay." If you live a bad life now, you may come back in another life as a beetle. And only when you have worked your passage through many lives, will you reach extinction. The Christian faith believes we have only one life and our destiny is not extinction but to know God and enjoy him forever. Unlike all the other faiths, it maintains that we are never going to be good enough for this great God, but that God in his amazing love has come to rescue us because he could not bear to have us separated from him forever by the many evil choices we have consciously made.

It will not do to pin our hopes on the baseless idea of all the roads leading up to the top of the same mountain. What if it is a false analogy? What if a better picture might be a maze, with lots of false turns in it and only one way to get out?

So how do we get any clear direction about the many religions? Here's a suggestion. Why not start with looking into whether Jesus Christ is reliable? After all, he has had more influence on the world than any other great teacher. We even date our calendar from the time of his birth. There really is no better way of finding out the truth than to look into the story of this amazing person for yourself. Anyone who does this will probably find four things that set Jesus apart from any of the great religious leaders of the world and make him incomparably the greatest.

First, no great religious teacher other than Jesus ever claimed to bring God before our gaze, let alone validate his claim by his life. C. S. Lewis expresses the difference well:

> There is no half-way house, and there is no parallel in other religions. If you had gone to Buddha and asked, "Are you the son of Bramah?" he would have said, "My son, you are still in the vale of illusion." If you had gone to Socrates and asked, "Are you Zeus?" he would have laughed at you. If you had gone to Muhammad and asked, "Are you Allah?" he would first have rent his clothes and then cut off your head.

In sharp contrast to these other great teachers, Jesus claimed that he and his heavenly Father were one, that if you wanted to see the Father you needed to take a long look at Jesus himself (see John 10:30; 14:7–10). He claimed, "No one knows the Father except the Son and anyone to whom the Son chooses to reveal him" (Matt. 11:27). And then he went on to invite his hearers to come not to the temple or to the law but to himself: "Come to me, all you that are weary and are carrying heavy burdens, and I will give you rest" (v. 28). Elsewhere he makes the most astonishing claims, that he is the way to God, the truth of God, the very life of God (John 14:6), that he is the bread without which we starve, and the wine without which we are parched (6:35; 15:1). We find him doing what the ancient Scriptures said only God could do, like stilling a mighty storm with a word (Mark 4:39), raising a dead person to new life (Luke 7:14–15), feeding a hungry multitude of five thousand with a few small loaves (Mark 6:38–44), or offering divine forgiveness—and healing—to a man who

71

had lain paralyzed for years (2:1–12). And Jesus backed his unique claims with unique deeds.

Second, nobody else among the great teachers has dealt satisfactorily with the problem of wickedness. Both Buddhism and Hinduism teach the inexorable law of karma. In another life you will bear the consequences for your misdeeds. Islam predicts the fires of hell for all non-Muslims (Qur'an 74.27–29; 50.24–26; 78.21–30). Even Muslims can never be sure of acceptance with God, for "Allah punishes whom he pleases and grants mercy to whom he pleases" (Qur'an 2.284). But Jesus's teaching on the subject was revolutionary. He said that he would give his life as a ransom to buy back the many who had been taken captive by evil (Mark 10:45). And on the cross, that is just what he did. He took personal responsibility for all the evil the world had done (see 1 Peter 2:24; 3:18). It broke his heart; it killed him. Because he was human like us, it was a human being paying the price, if you like. Because he was more than human, sharing God's nature, that offering of his is effective for all time (Heb. 10:14–18). Those who lived before Jesus and cast themselves on God's mercy, and those since his day who have done the same, all are accepted because not only is God love, but he is perfect justice as well (Rom. 3:24–26). The debt has been paid; the guilt has been purged or purified by his wonderful death on the cross that secured our pardon.

As if that were not enough, Jesus shows himself as the One you can really trust your life to because he is alive. The whole New Testament glows with the confidence that Jesus is alive.[1] He is the Easter Jesus. He came back from the cold. He broke the power of the last and greatest enemy, death. He is alive, never to die again. What confidence that very well-attested resurrection can give us! We have the assurance that he really is the Son of God, assurance that he really is the way to God, assurance that his teaching is truth, assurance that he can give us new life, both now and when we die. Nobody else among the religions of the world offers anything remotely comparable. No other great teacher came back from death as its conqueror. The bones of the Buddha are revered and divided up into 547 pieces among monasteries in Southeast Asia. The bones of Muhammad lie in Medina. But the bones of Jesus are nowhere to be found. As the first Christians put it, "We know that Christ, being raised from the dead, will never die again; death no longer has dominion over him" (Rom. 6:9). That fact alone would be sufficient to set him apart from all the other great teachers of the world.

The fourth thing that sets Jesus apart is the best of all. This Jesus offers to come and share the life of the believer. He is willing to come and be our constant companion, guide, and friend. He has promised, "I will never leave you or forsake you" (Heb. 13:5; see also Matt. 28:20).

So you see, it is not mere Christian prejudice that leads me to point you to Jesus. He offers these four great assurances that you can never find in any of the other religions of the world. So there is a lot of sense in recognizing that Christianity is not really a religion at all. Religion is something man-made, which is why there are so many of them. All of them offer their own way of attempting to get through to God. But the Christian gospel says that there is no way by which we can find God. He is too holy, pure, and upright—and we are not. He is so great and we are so small. There is no way through to him. But in his love he has made a way, a way back and a way in! Real Christianity is not a religion but a revelation—showing us what God is like, through the person, life, and death of Jesus.

73

It is also a rescue from the guilt and condemnation of the stuff in our past of which we are ashamed. Moreover, it is a relationship with him that lasts forever.

That does not mean that all other faiths have nothing helpful in them. They all have major strengths in their teachings, or they would never have attracted any worshipers. But if you want to get it sorted out for yourself, why not explore the One who came to earth for the very purpose of getting to know and love and help you? There's only one person like that!

9

"There's not enough proof for me to believe"

• •

Bernie, in his mid twenties, works in marketing. He has a degree in business studies and lives with friends in south London. His work is essentially about decision making—which campaigns should run using which media channels (television, radio, Internet, billboard, direct mail, and so on), for how long, and costing how much. It can be something of a minefield, he admits, with the best chance of success coming from gathering and analyzing the most accurate information—about consumer attitudes, media consumption, budgetary limitations—available.

With work, soccer, and socializing taking up the lion's share of his life, Bernie has little interest in matters religious or spiritual. He is earning good money, has lots of friends, is in good health, and has no "hole in his life" to be filled.

Actually he has little to say about religion. He knows very little about traditional religions, not enough to make him believe or disbelieve, so he describes himself as agnostic and admits he doesn't really want to make the effort to find out what is true.

He can, however, talk about the idea of believing which, in his work, is the word people often use when they don't really know the answer. When, for example, a colleague says that they believe that a brand's market penetration is X percent or that $Y is the right price point for a new product, his first question is what evidence do they have for their belief. If they have none, their belief is, as far as he is concerned, worthless. Belief on its own is just not good enough.

"I don't say that I don't believe in it. I don't say that I do believe it," he says. "I think until a proof has been shown to me, there are too many missing links." He is not entirely clear on what "it" is but he is sure that it is unproven and therefore unreliable. "A lot of it, I think, well all of it is unproven, so you don't know whether to believe in it or not."

When pressed on what proof he might want, it becomes clear that for him proof is actually synonymous with tangible evidence. "There's no concrete and no physical evidence, is there?" he says. "It's hard to believe anything when you can't actually prove it to yourself."

He seems to think that religious claims demand complete and unquestioning acquiescence and, in one unsure moment, refers to "doubting Thomas" to explain this: "In the Bible you've got the doubting Thomas thing, haven't you? That's their [religious people's] card, isn't it, to those people who don't believe, people who want evidence? Doubting Thomas—there's a little story to stop people wanting evidence all the time. It's wrong to want it; you've just got to believe it, you've got to have faith."

As far as Bernie is concerned, religious faith is untenable because it is not based on any evidence, certainly nothing like the research and statistics he deals with at work. Belief is unjustifiable because it is not proof.

●●●●

Nothing worthwhile in life is provable in the sense Bernie is after. Indeed no one can prove that his mother loves him or even that he is alive. There is good evidence for these things, of course, and we act on this evidence all the time.

In chapter 12 I deal with the nature of proof and the solid evidence that points to the existence of God. Nick Spencer's survey deliberately excluded people who were sure God existed and also those who were sure he did not. He concentrated on the great majority of the British population who currently do not go anywhere to worship and are negative or very unsure about the claims of the Christian faith. But I should be failing in my task if I did not go beyond his self-imposed limits and say something to those who are very dubious about the existence of God. In chapter 12 I offer seven facts, not theories or beliefs but seven facts, that point individually in the direction of God's reality, and when taken together, they make an overwhelming case—evidence—on which one can base a rational decision.

In this chapter I am going to turn to the evidence that Jesus is the Son of God. When we decide that he really is God's special messenger or representative who has come to show us what God is like and has gone to the anguish of crucifixion to bring us back to God, it changes our skeptical attitude. For people like Bernie, I want to offer evidence, because evidence is what they need.

Let's get it clear to begin with that Jesus is a historical figure. There is far more evidence for his existence than there is for Julius Caesar, for example. It is not only the Gospels and letters of the New Testament and an unbroken chain of writers since then that attest to this fact. Both Jewish and Roman writers of the time tell us about Jesus.

The Roman historian Tacitus, who wrote at the end of the first century, talks about the fire of Rome in AD 64 and rejects the idea that the Christians had started it. He says, "The name of Christians comes to them from Christ who was executed in the reign of Tiberius by the Procurator Pontius Pilate."[1] Pliny, writing a decade later, speaks of the enormous advance of the Christian cause in north Turkey where he was governor. He tells us that the only bizarre thing he could find about the Christians was that they met early in the morning and "sang a hymn to Christ as God," and they refused to bow down to the Emperor's statue and deny the name of Jesus.[2]

The Jewish author Josephus, writing at the end of the first century, has an astonishing piece about Jesus that is worth quoting, since it is so remarkable that a Jew wrote it.

> There arose about that time [Pilate's time, AD 26–36] Jesus, a wise man, if indeed we should call him a man, for he was a doer of marvellous deeds, a teacher of men who receive the truth with pleasure. He won over many Jews and also many Greeks. This man was the Messiah. And when Pilate had condemned him to the cross at the instigation of our own leaders, those who loved him from the first did not cease. For he appeared to them on the third day alive again, as the holy prophets had predicted and said many other wonderful things about him. And even now the race of Christians, so named after him, has not died out.[3]

Some people find these words so astounding coming from a Jew that they suspect he can't have written them. But they are in all copies of the text of Josephus!

So let's not pretend there is no secular evidence about Jesus. Actually, if you amass them all together, the sources give us a remarkable confirmation of what we read in the

Gospels. The secular and Jewish sources tell us that Jesus had a most remarkable birth. He had a brother called James. He worked miracles. He had disciples who were called Christians and who worshiped him as God. He said he would die and then return again. He was executed by Pilate, on a day when the sky turned black at Passover time. He rose from the tomb and was seen by his followers. Christianity rapidly spread to Rome, Alexandria, and Asia Minor and became a worldwide movement. His essential message was embodied in the letters of the Greek word for a fish meaning "Jesus Christ, Son of God, Savior," which was found all over the Roman Empire.

But of course the best evidence is the Gospels, which have come down to us from first-century companions of Jesus and their colleagues. In chapter 5 I discuss the overwhelming evidence that the Bible is truth and tells us that Jesus was a real person who brought God into our midst in terms we could really understand (the terms of a human life), that his death on the cross did all that was necessary to bring guilty folk like you and me back to God, and that he is alive again, gloriously alive. Otherwise, it would have been impossible for the church to get started. There were lots of so-called messiahs in the politically frenetic atmosphere of first-century Judea. The Romans executed them efficiently, their followers disappeared, and the whole thing was forgotten until the next one turned up. Not so with Jesus. This executed Galilean peasant teacher rose from the dead, and two thousand years later, more than a third of the world worships him as God.

The fact is that there is nothing wrong with the evidence. Many won't accept it because of the difference it will make in their lives. They are quite happy to remain as they are. One of these days, though, we are all going to die. Then the God who gave us life will call us to account for how we have used it, and we will face his judgment. The Bible says, "It is appointed for mortals to die once, and after that the judgment" (Heb. 9:27). It says, "All of us must appear before the judgment seat of Christ" (2 Cor. 5:10). It's not worth taking a chance on this not being true. Can we say to God, "Sorry I didn't bother about you. I did not think there was enough evidence"? Would God not be justified in replying: "I gave you the evidence of a beautiful world that I had made. I gave you the evidence of a moral conscience, pointing to me. I gave you the supreme evidence of my Jesus who came for you. He died for you, he is alive for you, and he has been asking for admission to your life for decades. And you tell me there is no evidence? You did not even bother to look into it, because you were so caught up in your soccer, your friends, and your comfortable lifestyle. You worked at advertising products that were soon out of date and checking consumer attitudes that were soon irrelevant. Whose fault is it that you simply did not bother to check out the evidence for the truth of the Christian story?"

If you decide that this story is true, then it is clearly the most important thing in the world. There is a God and he cares for you and looks for your response. But if you find it is not true, then feel free to discard it relentlessly. Attack Christianity for all you are worth! But don't remain satisfied to describe yourself as an agnostic who simply does not care enough to find out.

Bernie sees faith or belief as an inferior form of knowledge, but that is not what Christian faith is. It is not a poor substitute for knowledge at all. Faith means trust, like in a good marriage. As a matter of fact everyone has faith in something—in a partner, a theory such as the theory of evolution, or the chair he or she is sitting on. Each of these has an element of self-commitment about it, but only when the evidence warrants it.

Bernie mentions the story of Thomas, the doubter (John 20:24–29). Thomas didn't believe Jesus had been raised from the dead, and he didn't believe his friends who assured him that they had met the risen Jesus. Thomas wanted tangible evidence, and he got it. Jesus stood before him, with the marks of the nail wounds in his hands and the spear wound in his side, and said "Peace be with you." He wants to say the same to you and me. He invited Thomas to put his finger in the holes in his hands and his hand into the hole in his side and to throw away his doubts. He invited him to believe, to trust, to commit himself. I don't for a moment suppose Thomas had to touch Jesus's wounds. He was down on his face on the floor, no doubt weeping his eyes out, saying, "My Lord and my God!"

It is interesting that the author makes this incident the climax of his Gospel. A few verses later he tells us why. He recorded this very tangible proof among many other evidential signs in his Gospel for two reasons. He wanted his readers to "come to believe that Jesus is the Messiah, the Son of God." And he wanted them—and you—to go on from there and commit themselves to Jesus, so that "believing you may have life in his name" (v. 31). All agnostics need to get the Gospel of John on their reading lists!

10

"Something two thousand years old can't be relevant today"

Chloe has never known a world without personal computers, mobile phones, the Internet, multichannel television, DVDs, and video games. She has grown up in a "technotopia." Living without these gadgets is almost inconceivable to her.

Having recently turned twenty, she lives with her parents in a wealthy suburb of Nottingham and goes to college. She is excited by life and has a wide circle of friends, enough money to socialize, and the prospect of a good job when she graduates. Religious faith does not even feature on her radar.

It's not surprising that it takes quite an effort for her to talk about Christianity, not because she isn't intelligent but because she has never really thought about religion and has no real opinion about it. Her knowledge of Christianity (and indeed of all religions) is close to nonexistent. She knows Christianity is about God and about Jesus but that is about it. She has more to say when questioned about why she thinks so few people attend church these days.

"Religion is different for our generation than it was for older generations," she says. "They were perhaps brought up not to question things so much, so they would go to church because their parents told them to. We have been brought up to question society or question whatever and make up our own minds, so we are not so inclined to go to church without knowing why we should go."

She has a great deal of respect for her parents, but in her heart she believes that the world has moved too fast for them and their generation. Theirs was a world, she thinks, of credulousness and obedience, whereas hers is one of skepticism and rebellion. Without saying it in as many words, she feels their attitudes about life are pretty much out-of-date. This train of thought leads her back to the religious claims. If her parents' generation is already outdated, how much more are the beliefs of people who lived hundreds or thousands of years ago?

"A lot of the rules that were set out so many thousands of years ago are not really as relevant in today's society," she says. That was then, she believes. This is now. And while she is open-minded and nonjudgmental about whether such rules were a good thing at the time, it is inconceivable to her that they could possibly be relevant today.

"The story behind it all just doesn't interest me at all. It's just what I believe about here and now, you know."

●●●●

"That was then. This is now." That is a splendid and fairly typical attitude for a twenty year old who has money, friends, and good prospects. Chloe has never needed God and church. Her parents are well-meaning "oldies." They didn't have the wealth of information presented by the Internet or the adult toys that we have nowadays. It's interesting that the attitude of Chloe's generation is new. No previous generation has made so radical a disjunction between their age and what has gone before.

84

I confess I have a soft spot for the vitality, the self-confidence, and the gentle dismissiveness of such a worldview. But it really won't do, and I fancy that as Chloe grows older, she will find it simply isn't true. Major events in the past are relevant because they helped shape our present world. For example, we would not be able to go to the hospital for free were it not for the founding of the National Health Service sixty years ago. In any case, human nature is pretty much a constant throughout recorded history. Two thousand years ago the shape of society may have been very different, but human needs and concerns, hopes and fears, purpose and identity remain the same today. And real Christianity speaks to these concerns just as much as it did two thousand years ago.

Skepticism, though certainly characteristic of the younger generations, was there among the ancient Greeks six hundred years before Christ, and has been a major mark of European thought since Descartes in the seventeenth century. It lies at the heart of scientific method. It simply means we are determined to evaluate evidence critically and not be taken for a ride by believing in myths. And that makes admirable sense.

It is a mistake to imagine that something that occurred two thousand years ago could not be of relevance to you. The present is shaped by the past. The big bang is estimated to have taken place between five and fifteen billion years ago, and yet it has such impact on our lives that had it not happened, neither would we! However, an event long ago in the past, if it was *just* an event in the past, is indeed irrelevant to young people today. But an event that, like the big bang, has continued impact on all subsequent life is far from irrelevant. Christians claim that the coming, dying, and rising of the Son of God is comparable to the big bang.

It is God's act of re-creation and, like the big bang, has a lasting impact on all who have come after.

For many, like Chloe, who have had no experience of Christianity, they just "know it is about God and Jesus but that is about it." There is rather more to it than that. How could we ever know about God, whether he exists, and what he is like? There is no sure way, unless he came to show us. Christians down through the centuries have believed, on good evidence, which we looked at in chapter 9, that God has done just that. Jesus is not merely a wonderful man but the human embodiment of God, as much of God, if you like, as could be crammed into human form. His matchless life, his unparalleled teaching, his staggering claims, his fulfillment of scores of ancient prophecies, his love for one and all, his purity, his self-sacrifice all substantiate that claim. But there is one clinching argument. The apostle Paul, himself a reluctant convert from bloodthirsty opposition to Jesus Christ, alludes to it in his letter to Roman Christians. Jesus, he claims, was powerfully defined as the Son of God by his resurrection from the dead (Rom. 1:4). That resurrection, if it is true, sets him apart from all other great religious teachers throughout history. He predicted, so the Gospels tell us, that he would be cruelly mistreated, be crucified, and rise again from the dead (Mark 10:33–34). And it happened. All of Christian faith is built on the truth of the resurrection of Jesus Christ from the grip of death on the first Easter day.

If the resurrection of Jesus Christ is true, he is alive forevermore, alive for each of us personally. He can be our companion through life, our guide, our friend and will welcome us when the cold waters of death close over us. If this is true, it is profoundly relevant. But is it? This is where young people need to use their proclivity for being critical.

When I was a successful and confident teenager, I heard an old man solemnly telling a group of my peers, gathered in a sports pavilion, that Jesus Christ was alive. I thought it was ridiculous, and I asked who the speaker was. I found out he was the professor of surgery at Bristol University and the editor of the *British Medical Journal*! I realized that he could not be nuts. If he was persuaded that Jesus is alive, I had at least to look into it. I did. And I could not help being persuaded. In due course I entrusted myself to Christ, and since then companionship with the risen Jesus has profoundly changed my life.

It has been like that with countless people I have known. One good example is a car thief who came to Christ when lying in a pool of blood after being beaten up by the guards in prison. He cried out "God, help me!" and God did! Shortly afterward, the prison chaplain came in and showed him the way to Jesus. In due course, a couple of years after his release, he was accepted by the Church of England for training as a clergyman, and he came to the college where I was the principal. He had a very colorful and effective way of explaining the gospel and was ordained to work in a rough mining district in Nottinghamshire. His whole life was transformed. As a crook his great aim had been to get something for nothing. His new goal as a Christian minister was to earn a wage to sustain his family, offer hospitality to others, and introduce them to the Jesus who had changed his life. That's the sort of difference Jesus Christ makes when you put yourself into his hands.

So Jesus can be very relevant today, but can we really believe he rose from the dead? Is it possible that he is alive and able to help us today? Let's take a look at the evidence.

Contemporary accounts in the four Gospels and in the letters of the apostles Paul, Peter, and John make it abundantly clear that Jesus was crucified in a very public execution on the cross. He was placed in a rock-hewn tomb, the tomb was sealed up, and soldiers guarded it. This seems to have been because the various hints of resurrection Jesus had given throughout his ministry might have encouraged grave robbers to steal the body and claim he had risen. As a matter of fact a few people have made claims like this, notably Hugh Schonfield in his book *The Passover Plot*. But the idea that a crucified man could revive in the cool of the tomb and be spirited away, despite a rock at the entrance and a guard outside, is preposterous. We actually know for sure he was dead. Not only because Romans were expert at the grisly task of crucifixion and nobody ever survived but because one of the Gospel writers mentioned something amazing that he could not understand. When a spear was thrust under the heart of Jesus to make sure he was dead, out came "blood and water" (John 19:33–35). The science of the day was not advanced enough to explain that the separation of dark red clot from light colored serum is the strongest proof of death! So the resurrection is strongly supported by the fact that the tomb was found empty on the first Easter day, the third after his execution. What's more, the winding sheet packed with spices that had been put around his body was still there, along with the turban that wound around his head (20:6–7). Jesus was gone. He had been raised into a new form of existence. Who would have left the grave clothes all wound around like an empty chrysalis case if they had stolen the body?

The evidence for the resurrection does not depend, however, on an empty tomb but on a living Jesus, a Jesus whom people met after his resurrection, and there were hundreds of them, people who knew him well—the fishermen, the women who had accompanied his mission, his close associates. Our earliest account of the resurrection mentions "more than five hundred brothers and sisters" who saw him on a single occasion. Most of them, we read, were still alive when the record was penned in the early fifties AD, though some had died (1 Cor. 15:6). None of them was easily taken in. There is a note of initial incredulity in all the accounts, as you will see if you read the resurrection story in the four Gospels. But they were persuaded, and once persuaded they could not keep quiet. Nothing like this had ever been known since the foundation of the world. They had found the key to life! It's interesting that one of Jesus's disciples, Thomas, was absent the first time Jesus appeared to the others. He flatly disbelieved the story, but as we saw in chapter 9, Jesus appeared again, face-to-face with Thomas, and he fell down at the feet of Jesus with the strongest confession of faith to be found anywhere in the New Testament, "My Lord and my God!" (John 20:28). Or think of Saul of Tarsus, the scourge of Christians, who chased them from city to city and slaughtered them. That man, renamed Paul, became the strongest Christian evangelist there has ever been. And it happened because he met with the risen Christ and gratefully surrendered to him.

What fascinates me is the difference Christ made to such people. As we have just seen, the risen Jesus turned Saul of Tarsus from a bitter opponent to a joyful and passionate follower, who in due course gave his life for the cause of Christ. James, a brother in Jesus's family, did not believe in Jesus while he was alive, but after his death and resurrection, we find James leading the early church in Jerusalem. How come? Paul has a succinct answer to that: "he appeared to James" (1 Cor. 15:7). Simon Peter, the bombastic fisherman who was always talking big but achieving little during the days when Jesus was around, now, after the resurrection, becomes a man of rock, taking on the whole Jewish religious establishment. He fearlessly preached: "This Jesus God raised up, and of that all of us are witnesses" (Acts 2:32). These renewed followers of Jesus went and founded churches all over the Roman world. They were over the moon with their discovery that guilt and death did not hold all the aces. On the contrary, their Jesus had trumped the lot. He had dealt with evil by taking its consequences on himself. He was alive forevermore, the conqueror of death and companion of those who would trust him. And the more you persecuted these Christians and killed them, the more the movement spread. Precisely the same thing is happening today in places like Tanzania, China, Nigeria—to name but three. The risen Jesus Christ can be known and enjoyed by anyone, and today the Christian gospel is spreading worldwide faster than it ever has before. People who have met Jesus cannot keep quiet about him.

What Christ has done is not all about some event in the past that is irrelevant to us today. The dynamic impact of that historic event remains. The tomb was empty. Jesus rose from the dead and he met lots of people. He changed their lives, giving them a tremendous new joy, moral power, and courage, together with a glorious hope beyond death. Listen to Simon Peter on the subject: "Blessed be the God and Father of our Lord Jesus Christ! By his great mercy he has given us a new birth into a living hope through the resurrection of Jesus Christ from the dead" (1 Peter 1:3). And it was not just that first generation on which Jesus had such an impact. He has been doing it ever since. He has done it for me. I have seen him make contact with people on every continent and start changing their lives for the better. There is no reason why he should not do it for you, if only you will ask him to come and start living in you. We may be excited by life, but until we get linked up with the life of Jesus, we have no idea how fulfilling life can be.

11

"If there is a God, why doesn't he send someone to help us?"

Of all of the different reasons for unbelief discussed in the various interviews, one in particular came up most often and was most intensely felt. Few of those interviewed expressed more than a handful of the sentiments discussed so far, and for many of those there was a tension between what they wanted to believe and what they thought was credible. "My head tells me there isn't a God, but my heart wants to believe in it," one explained. "Without having that higher plane or greater being, you'd never have hope. Hope would be pointless. Why would you hope or wish for something?" asked another. In spite of this yearning, the reasons not to believe were, at least for this group of people, too strong, with the most difficult problem being that of suffering.

As already noted, people's attitude to suffering varied, some blaming God for everything, some blaming him for natural disasters, some blaming human beings for most things, some blaming religion in particular.

Underlying many of the complaints and intellectual problems was a personal, emotional issue. The problem was at least as much about the way the heart feels as the way the mind thinks. And in spite of recognizing the cause of at least some of the world's suffering, those who were interviewed had little to suggest about what should be done, short of demanding peace rather than war, and tolerance rather than intolerance.

In the midst of such discussions, God was criticized and "called on" several times, with one of the most poignant moments being when someone, earnestly and almost desperately said, "There's so much war and conflict. If there is a God, why doesn't he just send someone down to help us?"

● ● ● ●

These comments are cries from the heart. How right it is to observe that without having a higher plane or a greater being to look to, we can have no lasting hope. Short-term hopes are possible, but in the end, if there is no God, all our hopes will crumble to ashes with the approach of death. Shakespeare would be right in seeing life as "a tale told by an idiot, full of sound and fury, signifying nothing." Hope is one of the most fundamental characteristics of life. Without hope we cannot live fulfilled lives.

But what about this poignant hope that there might be a God who could send someone down to help us? Is this just one more hope doomed to come to nothing? "My head tells me there isn't a God, but my heart wants to believe in it" was the cry. But does our head really tell us there is no God? Do we really have to throw our brains away if we become Christians? In the final chapter of this book I offer you a number of solid facts, which point very clearly to the existence and nature of God. But in this chapter I'd like to take a different tack.

Just suppose for a moment that the vast majority of humankind across the world and down the ages is right, and there is a God, a supreme source of our world and of ourselves, from whom all else flows. Take a flight of imagination and think what it would be like if you yourself were this God. Now what would you do if you wanted to reach out in love to the human beings you had made in your own likeness but who did not want to know you? How would you get through to men and women in revolt, who were convinced you did not exist?

To begin with, you have already created a marvelous *world*, which shouts out the love, skill, power, and beauty of the Creator. Well, perhaps God has done just that.

And you have already created *people* who are capable of responding to love. You chose to give people the dangerous gift of free will, so they are able either to respond to you or to reject you. Well, maybe God has taken the risk and has done that too.

You have already instilled in the hearts of these people *values* that speak of God, values like truth, goodness, beauty, harmony, creativity, and love. Of course you can never force virtue on them. As free agents, they can choose the opposite—and people often do. But wherever they are found, these qualities point to the Giver, the One who is absolute truth, perfect goodness, unutterable beauty, complete harmony, unceasing creativity, and the very source of love. Such qualities are the imprint of God. God has done this as well.

You might like the idea of building in a *conscience*, which would alert your creatures to right and wrong, a conscience that approves good choices and prods and warns against anything that strays from your will, which is no arbitrary whim but encompasses their highest good. This conscience would persevere no matter how much they tried to stifle it. Could God have done that too?

95

Then you could instill *a God-shaped blank* into their lives, a hole that nothing else could fill apart from God himself, a space that cries out for satisfaction and fulfillment despite the rubbish that people stuff into it, a space that would elicit from them the cry that came to Augustine's lips centuries ago: "O God, you have made us for yourself, and our hearts are restless until they find their rest in you." God has done that too, has he not? Someone said, "My heart wants to believe in it."

You might then, if you were God, show your hand in the *course of history*. You might ensure that the arrogance of nations and civilizations led inevitably to corruption and fall. You might concentrate on one man to begin with, then one family, one tribe, one nation that would trust you and obey you, a people that in time you could train to receive and perhaps even follow your directions for their highest good. They might have to go through war and captivity as they learn these lessons, but because the stakes were high, you would persevere with them and take great pains to lead them. So much would depend on their understanding and their lifestyle if you were going to be able to really get through to them and then through them to reach out to a whole lost world that was out of touch with you. Isn't that precisely what God did with the Jewish people in the centuries leading up to Christ?

Finally, it's conceivable that you would decide to *come in person* to their world. You would have to come as one of them, of course, for if you disclosed yourself in all your radiant beauty, the sight would blind them. You would need to arrive softly and in disguise. You would need to learn their language so perfectly, without the trace of a foreign accent, that you could easily be mistaken for a native. It would be immensely costly. You would have to love them an awful lot if you were going to shrink yourself down to their level. It would be rather like one of us voluntarily turning into a rat or a slug, for the purpose of communicating effectively with such lowly creatures. It would be an almost unthinkable sacrifice. But what if God did that too?

And if your love for them is boundless, you might even take one further step, *rescue*. Remember, they are out of touch with you, because of the wrong things they have thought and done and the wrong attitude they have toward you. That must matter to you. All is not well, and you can't pretend that it is. They are guilty of wrongdoing. They are cut off. But have you taken all that trouble to get in touch with them only to leave them in the lurch? Surely not. You will come to the rescue, cost what it may.

Long ago you made it clear that if humans determine to cut themselves off from you, you will ratify their choice. They will get what they want. You will respect their freedom to choose, even if it's the choice of hell. But if you were utterly determined to broker reconciliation, you might determine to bear the punishment for these people, to die on their behalf, to carry in your own person the guilt that everyone shares, to pay the ransom price to set people free. The precise imagery is comparatively unimportant. However, the fact—if true—is the most important in all the world. There is a living God and he loves his people enough to die for them! Could God have done that too?

It was the conviction that God had done precisely this, which fired up the early Christians. At first they were only a handful of ordinary men and women, but in due course they engulfed the Roman Empire and became the largest religion the world has ever seen, embracing a third of humankind and still growing with many thousand new believers every day. The longing of the hearts of these Christians was matched by the confidence of their minds. The Great Lover, the Great Reconciler had come. He had died for them. He was alive for them. They knew him. And there was nothing so important as to revel in that relationship and pass it on to others.

In the last two chapters we have looked at some of the evidence for who Jesus is and for his resurrection from the dead. Surely now is the time for you to respond to this evidence. You will always be torn between heart and head until you surrender yourself to the God who gave you both. If you want the longings of your heart and the workings of your mind to come together in a harmonious balance, there is a step to be taken, a step that cannot be avoided. It is to come back to God and admit that you have kept him out of your life. Admit that your attitude of independence from him has led to bad things in your behavior, your habits, and your relationships. There is no way that we can approach a holy God without a genuine "Sorry" on our lips—and in our hearts.

I think you will find that your "sorry" leads to real joy and gratitude too. By now you have realized that what I asked you to imagine is no dream but solid reality, so solid that you could have bruised your toes on the cradle in Bethlehem or got splinters in your hand from the cross at Calvary. And you will want to thank God with all your heart that he has bothered about you, come for you, died for you, and is alive for you. Indeed, at the end of your road, he will welcome you home. You know it won't be easy to be a follower of Jesus, a real Christian, in a society that often ignores him, but you are prepared for that. Of course you will need to team up with other followers of Jesus. But first and foremost, you need to tell him that you are gladly accepting his most gracious offer: "Listen! I am standing at the door, knocking; if you hear my voice and open the door, I will come in" (Rev. 3:20). You have heard his voice in your heart—yes, and in your mind as well. Do you long to experience for yourself the reality of a relationship with God? Then invite the Lord to come and share your very being. Ask his unseen risen life, his Holy Spirit, to come into your life, just as you would invite a friend to enter your home. "Come in," you would say, as you unlock the door. "Great to see you. Sorry about the mess. Have some coffee." The words in Revelation 3:20 make it crystal clear that the Lord himself will come in, he will accept your hospitality, and he will never leave you. And as for the mess—why, he is the man with the vacuum cleaner!

12

"I'm still not sure I believe in God"

Let's remind ourselves where these varied objections to the Christian faith have taken us. The climate of our society is decidedly post-Christian, so it is very understandable that many people do not take the time and trouble to look into the claims of Christianity. They see no reason to do so, because the image they have of the church is unattractive. After all, we want to make the most of life, and the church seems so inflexible and dull. We want to express ourselves, and the church doesn't cater to that. Its services seem dominated by a predetermined pattern.

I've already acknowledged that people can be spiritual without going to church and that some churchgoers seem to be hypocrites. There is some truth to these objections, but they are not compelling.

We looked at the question of tolerance, almost the only virtue that is still admired today. And we have seen that if Christians seem intolerant, it is usually because of their loyalty to the teaching of Jesus Christ, so their intolerance in this sense should be understandable.

Then we moved on to some very substantive issues. Can we trust the Bible? Has science disproved Christianity? What about the problems of suffering and the multiplicity of religions in the world? And is evidence for the life, death, and resurrection of Jesus Christ solid enough to warrant our allegiance? We reflected on the limitations of proof. We examined the very modern idea that if something is old it cannot be relevant and found this idea to be a mistake. And finally we responded to the marvelous question, "If there is a God, why doesn't he just send someone down to help us?" There is only one faith in the world that claims God has done just that. It is the Christian faith.

But I suspect that, although we may appreciate the responses that have been given to these questions that haunt many people's minds, there is that lurking suspicion that there may not be enough evidence for us to believe in God at all. So before I shut down my computer, I want to say something to you who are tending toward atheism, because it seems to be the most likely explanation of ourselves and our world.

If you go by television programs or the conversations in the pub, you might think that there are a large number of people in Britain who are atheists. As a matter of fact the number is rather small, a mere 10 percent in the 1998 survey done by the Office for National Statistics. Statistics cannot determine the truth or otherwise of belief in God, but at least they show that, compared with atheists, believers are not a tiny remnant.

Let's begin by reminding ourselves again of the limited usefulness of proof. You can neither prove God nor disprove him. You can't prove your partner loves you. In fact there are precious few things you can prove, and they are by no means the most interesting aspects of life. To prove a thing means to show that it could not be otherwise, and that is a very final form of certainty. You cannot prove the sun will rise tomorrow. You cannot actually prove that you are alive. You cannot prove you are the same person you were ten years ago. The philosopher David Hume attempted to prove the link between himself and the man he was ten years previously, and he utterly failed! Proof applies only to rarified areas of mathematics and philosophy. For the rest, we have to work on good evidence. There is very good evidence for our existence, for our identity, and for supposing that the sun will rise tomorrow. And there is good reason to believe in God. Indeed, the evidence is so good that it is much harder to reject God's existence than to accept it.

Very well, let's have a look at the evidence. I am not going to offer you theories or impressions but facts. Let us see where they point.

The Fact of the World

Reflect on the world. So far as we know at present, this planet is the only part of the universe where there is conscious life. What accounts for this world of ours? Most scientists have abandoned the steady state theory of the origin of the universe in favor of the big bang. But we can't leave it there. We cannot help asking what lay behind the big bang. What caused it? If the answer is in terms of atoms, molecules, and DNA, the question must be pressed, why should they possess the remarkable properties they do? Why should there be any atoms rather than none? And why should DNA be the individual and unique key to everybody on earth? We all know that nothing comes from nothing. Every finite thing is caused. To put it in philosophical terms, all contingent facts must, in the final analysis, be based on a necessary cause. If you deny that, you have real problems in suggesting how this highly sophisticated world originated.

You may say that evolution is the answer. That will scarcely do. Even if the theory of evolution were universally accepted among scientists, you would need to have an adequate starting point for the evolutionary process. Darwin himself, at the beginning of *On the Origin of Species*, acknowledged God as that source. And we can't escape from the necessity of God by saying, "Well, it is sheer chance. Just one of those things." If the world was due to chance, why are cause and effect built into it at every turn? It is not very rational to suppose that chance gives rise to cause and effect. And it is not very rational to suggest that the world that is based on cause and effect is itself uncaused. Huxley once said, "The link between cause and effect is the chief article of the scientist's creed." "If you think hard enough," said the Oxford biologist Professor Sir Alister Hardy, "science itself drives you back to belief in a Creator."

The Fact of Design

Reflect on the fact of design in the world. At every level nature shows evidence of design. Think of the focusing equipment of the eye, the intricacy of the ear, the radar of a bat, the built-in gyroscope of a swallow, or the camouflage of a pheasant. Or think of the perfect harmony of the laws of physics. Reflect on the marvel of conception and birth. At every point there is evidence of a great Designer. Modern science is recognizing this as the anthropic principle.

It means that had the circumstances of our physical world been a fraction different, life could not have existed on this planet, which seems to be custom-made for human life! As Professor John Polkinghorne put it, "There is a very tight-knit series of constraints . . . on the way our world must be in order that we are here to observe it." Even John Stuart Mill, a strong opponent of Christianity, came to this conclusion at the end of his life: "The argument from design is irresistible," he said. "Nature does testify to its Creator." Professor Paul Davies, the distinguished New Zealand physicist, writes: "The well-defined laws of physics, and definite cause and effect relationships, reveal a level of order and symmetry in the universe that demand some sort of cosmic design." Einstein, too, spoke of his "humble admiration of the illimitably superior Spirit who reveals himself in the slight details which we can perceive with our frail minds."

Physicists operate on the assumption of consistency and design in the universe. Very well, if there is design, where did it come from? Not from us. We don't lay down the laws of nature or design the development of the fetus in the womb. It very much looks as if a Designer is at work. The argument from design is highly persuasive, and to say with Jean-Paul Sartre, "This world is not the product of intelligence. It meets our gaze as would a crumpled piece of paper. . . . What is man but a little puddle of water whose freedom is death?" is to shut your eyes to one of the clearest indications that there is a Creator God who has not left himself without witness. "The heavens are telling the glory of God; and the firmament proclaims his handiwork" (Ps. 19:1) remains true; so does the Bible's assertion, "Fools say in their hearts, 'There is no God'" (14:1).

The Fact of Personality

Look at the fact of personality. It is one of the most remarkable phenomena in the world. The difference between a person and a thing, between a live person and a dead one, is fundamental. When Sartre, in the quotation given above, denied that the world was created by Intelligence, he was not only insulting his Maker, but he was insulting his own powers of reasoning. He was saying in effect that there was no reason to believe what he was saying! The fact is that we are not mere robots; there is more to us than that. We have human personality.

No doubt the medical student can analyze his girlfriend into calcium, water, fat, and so forth. But he chooses her for other reasons—because she is a person he admires. You cannot reduce love and emotions, resolve and decision-making to chemistry. We are not mere matter. But the alternative is disturbing. It suggests that my personality cannot be explained simply in terms of its physical components alone. I am more than matter. But how could that be if there is no God? Can a craftsman create something more skilled than himself? Of course not. Then how—according to the atheistic view—do we get human personality out of the inorganic matter that is the brute stuff of which our universe is exhaustively composed? Can rationality and life spring from chance and nonbeing? No, the fact of human personality is another impressive pointer to the God who created us in his own image. That is not to say that God is restricted to a personality like ours, but it is to say that the ultimate source of our being is not less than personal. Paul Davies, not himself a Christian, makes this point well:

> The physical species *homo sapiens* may count for nothing,
> but the existence of mind in some planet in the universe is

surely a fact of fundamental importance. This is no trivial detail, no minor by-product of mindless purposeless forces. We are truly meant to be here. The physical universe is put together with an ingenuity so astonishing that I cannot accept it merely as brute fact. There must be a deeper level of explanation.

Where else can we look for that deeper level of explanation for mind and personhood in our world than to God?

The Fact of Values

Look at the fact of values. We all have them, but they are very hard to understand if there is no God. After all, you don't expect to find values knocking around in molecules! Matter does not give rise to morals. So modern godless people are confused about where our values fit in. We value life, but why should we, if life really springs from chance? We value truth, but why should we, if there is no ultimate reality? We value goodness, but what is that doing in a world derived from plankton? We revel in beauty, but there is nothing in it, since it too springs from the chaos in which our world originated. We value communication, but the universe is silent. Yes, we have our values, and they do not accord very well with the atheist's picture of the world, sprung merely from chance, matter, and millions of years to allow for extensive development. I do not find much basis for value judgments there.

But what if there is a Creator God? Then life is valuable because it is his greatest gift and thus graces every individual with infinite value. Truth matters because it is one aspect of God, the ultimate reality. Beauty and goodness are likewise two of the "faces" of God, and every good action or beautiful sight is an inkling of the good and beautiful source from which they come. Best of all, we do not inhabit a silent planet. God has spoken and revealed himself, to a considerable extent, in the world and in its design, values, and human beings. When we communicate, it is not vain jabbering but God-given ability, entrusted to us by the great Communicator himself.

The Fact of Conscience

Look at the fact of conscience. That's a pointer to God if ever there was one. Your conscience does not argue. It acts like a lawmaker inside you, acquitting you or condemning you. It doesn't say, "Do this because you will gain by it" or "Do it because you will escape trouble that way." It just says, "Do it." It seems to be a remarkable, categorical pointer to the moral God who put it there. Oh, of course, it is not the voice of God pure and simple. It has been warped by all kinds of things: our environment, our rationalizations, our disobedience. But it is equally certain that conscience can't just be explained away as the pressure of society. It was not from any pressure by society that John Newton and William Wilberforce conscientiously fought for the liberation of slaves or that Martin Luther King championed the cause of black people. Their actions were carried out despite the opposition of society, and so it has always been with every moral advance.

Despite the diversity of human cultures the world over, there is actually remarkable agreement on the essential values to which conscience points: the general condemnation of murder and adultery, of theft and lust, of hate and hijacking. There is universal agreement that peace is right and war is wrong, that love is right and hate is wrong—however little we manage to carry it out in practice. And it is conscience that points us to this difference between right and wrong and the claim right has on us. C. S. Lewis summed it up like this: "If no set of moral ideas were better than another, there would be no sense in preferring civilized morality to Nazi morality. The moment you say one lot of morals is better than another, you are in fact measuring them by some ultimate standard." And that ultimate standard is God.

Morality, conscience, the difference between right and wrong are important pointers to a God who is interested in what is right and good and true. Here is no blind force, no abstruse designer, but a personal God, so concerned with what is right that he has built a moral compass into each one of his creatures.

The Fact of Religion

Look at the fact of religion. We are religious animals. In the sixth century BC philosophers in Greece poured scorn on religion and invited people to grow out of such superstition. Religion continued. And so it has done ever since. The Russians tried to abolish religion after the revolution in 1917. They failed. They tried again with violent persecution under Stalin. They failed. And now the gospel is making massive advances in Russia. Fifty years ago sociologists confidently predicted that religion would have withered away by the end of the twentieth century. Instead, it is the major force dominating world politics. The fact is that people are incurably religious. We are going to worship either God or a pseudo-God, but worship something we will, even if it is something very physical like material prosperity or something very abstract like the idea of progress.

> There is one fact about man that has distinguished him since his first appearance on earth. It marks him as different from all other creatures. That is, he's a worshipping animal. Wherever he has existed there are the remains, in some form or other, of his worship. That's not a pious conclusion: it's an observed fact. And all through history and prehistory when he's deprived himself of that he's gone to pieces. Many people nowadays are going to pieces, or they find the first convenient prop to tie their instincts to. It's behind the extraordinary adulation of royalty. It's behind the mobbing of TV stars. If you don't give expression to an instinct, you've got to sublimate it or go out of your mind.[1]

Such is the conclusion not of a philosopher or a priest but of novelist Winston Graham. He is right, is he not?

These are some of the facts that, taken together, not only make belief in God reasonable but make it very hard to deny his existence. They point to a God who is skillful, skillful enough to design the courses of the stars and the development of the fetus. They point to a God who is the source of human personality and therefore not less than personal, however much he may transcend all that we mean by that word. He is the source of our values—life, language, truth, beauty, and goodness find their ultimate home in him. He is so concerned about right and wrong that he has furnished each of his creatures with a conscience. And he wants us to know him, enjoy him, worship him, and live in his company, hence the universal religious instinct of men and women throughout history and all over the world. But he still remains the unknown God, unless he discloses himself. And that he has done.

110

The Fact of Jesus

The most compelling reason to believe in the existence of God is Jesus of Nazareth. He claimed to make God known. He claimed that to know him was to know the Father. He claimed to be empowered by his heavenly Father to forgive sins, to accept worship, and to be the final judge of humankind at the end of all history. He claimed that he would die for the sins of the world and would be raised to an endless life after tasting death for every man. All this is clearly before us on the pages of the Gospels. As we have seen in chapter 9, Jewish and Roman sources substantiate the existence of Jesus and a good deal about him.

The Gospels show that he lived a matchless life, taught as no man has ever taught, fulfilled scores of prophecies uttered centuries before, and yes, he was raised after death from the chill of the tomb on the first Easter day—what the great ancient historian Mommsen called "the best attested fact in ancient history." We glanced at some of the evidence for his resurrection in chapter 10.

To put it succinctly, if you examine the following eight factors, you will get to the heart of who Jesus is. His worldwide influence, his marvelous teaching, his moral perfection, his miracles, his fulfillment of prophecy, his claims, his death, and his resurrection add up to a formidable case that he is indeed the Son of God, the Savior of the world.

Conclusion

So you don't have to throw your brains away to become a believer in God. The evidence is very strong, far stronger than the atheist's case. Consider the alternative for a moment.

One of the most pressing questions of the twenty-first century is this: What is man? Christians believe that men and women are made in the image of God, and their inherent value lies in precisely this fact. Despite our frailty and failures, we remain the objects of God's love, and he plans to spend eternity with us.

But once we remove God, it all looks very different. Human beings do not spring from a loving personal source. As the atheist and Nobel Prize winner Jacques Monod put it, "Man must wake up to his total solitude, his fundamental isolation. Like a gypsy he lives on the boundary of an alien world, a world that is deaf to his music, and is as indifferent to his hopes and fears as to his sufferings and his crimes."

Consequently human beings have no inherent value. From matter we come and to matter we return. "Man has no divinely prepared nature to be fulfilled by action," wrote Sartre with rigorous frankness. "What is he but a little puddle of water whose freedom is death?" Ernest Hemingway wrote: "Life is just a dirty trick from nothingness to nothingness." And nothingness, of course, is where it all ends. "On humanist assumptions life leads nowhere, and every pretence that it does is a cruel deceit," wrote the very honest humanist H. J. Blackman.

And while he does remain alive, the modern atheist perceives in his own life and in society an increasing collapse in ethics. "Is there no God? Then everything is permitted," reflected Dostoyevsky. So it is not altogether surprising that Klaus Barbie, the notorious World War II "Butcher of Lyons," could claim, "I have done no wrong!" If you do not believe in a personal, ethical source of the world and all that is in it, then nobody should be surprised if moral behavior gives way to selfish gratification. Ethics becomes simply what I want or think I can get away with. This often happens in individual lives, but it has happened on a massive scale in the past century in the atheistic regimes of Hitler's Germany, Stalin's Russia, and Mao's China. Atheism set out to be the liberator of humankind. It emerged in Europe with the French Revolution at the end of the eighteenth century. It was a protest against the corruption of the church and the oppression of the monarchy. But almost immediately the admirable atheistic ideals of liberty, equality, and fraternity turned into the mindless slaughter of the Reign of Terror. And sadly in our own day, we have come to recognize that it is atheism not Christianity that has turned out to be the oppressor of humankind. Atheistic regimes have proved unbelievably oppressive and ruthless throughout the vast territories, amounting to nearly half the world, where they held sway fifty years ago. Millions have been slaughtered for daring to question their dogmas. But the Christian faith has been seen to be the liberator in the Soviet empire and most recently in China, where there are now well over seventy million believers. And this is no accident, for real Christianity makes intellectual sense of the world and of ourselves, and sharing our lives with the Author of our existence brings great joy, fosters love for other people, reaches out to meet human need, demands moral living, and offers a firm hope for life after death based on the historical resurrection of Jesus of Nazareth. I would not trade my Christian faith for anything this world has to offer, certainly not for the atheist's alternative.

It is hardly surprising that reflecting on the implications of rejecting God leads many thoughtful people to despair. "Only on the foundation of unyielding despair can the soul's habitation safely be built," claimed Bertrand Russell, that massively erudite atheistic philosopher. And today's postmodern generation tends to agree. The logic is inescapable. If there is no God, there is no ultimate hope for humankind. No wonder our society, like the Roman Empire in its decline and fall, is consumed with a desire for handouts from the state and exotic entertainment from the media. They dull the pain of a Godless world, but they cannot satisfy. Only God can do that.

Appendix

· ·

In his fascinating book *Beyond Belief?* Nick Spencer, a researcher, explains his examination of the religious views of agnostics. He moderated five groups of eight respondents, diverse in age, gender, and social background. Three groups were recruited in London, two in Nottingham, all by professional market research recruiters. The object of the research was to understand the attitudes of the agnostic mainstream that makes up the majority of our population.

Interviewees were recruited according to three main criteria: their (non)belief, their (non)attendance at religious services, and their self-designation (whether they called themselves Christians or not). People who were confident that God exists were excluded, as were those who were confident that there is no God. The remaining "agnostic" sample covered 66 percent of the population of Great Britain, according to the Office for National Statistics' *Social Trends 30*.

To establish the first criterion, recruiters read out to respondents a series of statements drawn from the 1998 British Social Attitudes survey:

1. I know God really exists, and I have no doubt about it.
2. While I have doubts, I feel I do believe in God.
3. I find myself believing in God some of the time but not at others.
4. I don't believe in a personal God but I do believe in a Higher Power of some kind.
5. I don't know whether there is a God and I don't believe there is any way of finding out.
6. I don't believe in God.

Then people were asked whether they regularly attended a religious service of any kind. Those who did were excluded. The rest belonged to the 81 percent of the population of Great Britain who, according to the Office for National Statistics' *Social Trends 31* (1999) do not worship as often as once a month.

Finally, people were asked about how they would describe themselves—Christian, Jew, Muslim, and so on. In the three London groups, all those who claimed to be part of one of these groups were excluded. This was modified in the Nottingham groups, because recruiters reported that there was a great willingness among people, despite being agnostic and nonattenders, to call themselves Christians. Though confusing, this is a common phenomenon. The 2001 National Census showed that 72 percent of the population of England and Wales call themselves Christian, and a further 5 percent belong to other religions. Only 16 percent said they had no religion (7 percent gave no answer). Thus both the London and Nottingham groups represent the enormous fringe constituency, which continues to exist in Britain. The Nottingham groups did not go to church, were not sure quite what they believe, but still liked to call themselves Christians, while the London groups came from the more antagonistic end of the agnostic spectrum. These were the respondents that Nick spoke to as part of his research. They were interviewed according to the three criteria outlined above, in two-hour groups, and were asked about their lives, beliefs, and attitudes toward religion in general and Christianity and the church in particular. Some of their responses are contained in the chapters in this book; the rest are in Nick's book *Beyond Belief?* obtainable from the London Institute for Contemporary Christianity (www.licc.org.uk). As Mark Greene, the director of the London Institute, observes, the results "afford a fascinating perspective on early twenty-first-century Britain."

Notes

• •

Chapter 6 "Science has disproved Christianity"

1. Alister McGrath, *The Twilight of Atheism: The Rise and Fall of Disbelief in the Modern World* (New York: Doubleday, 2004).

2. I am indebted to my colleague Professor Alister McGrath (distinguished scientist and theologian) for this quotation from Stephen J. Gould, *Scientific American* 267 (1992), 118–21, as well as for some other insights in this chapter.

Chapter 8 "All the religions in the world can't be true"

1. See, for example, the resurrection accounts in Matthew 28; Luke 24; John 20; 1 Corinthians 15.

Chapter 9 "There's not enough proof for me to believe"

1. Tacitus, *Annals*, 15.44.

2. Pliny, *Letters*, 10.96.

3. Josephus, *Antiquities*, 18.3.

Chapter 12 "I'm still not sure I believe in God"

1. Winston Graham, *The Sleeping Partner* (London: Hodder and Stoughton, 1956).

Further Reading

Chapter 1 "You don't have to go to church to be spiritual"

Sire, James W. *The Universe Next Door: A Basic World View Catalog*, 4th ed. InterVarsity Press, 2004.

Chapter 2 "The church is just too inflexible"

Green, M., ed. *Church without Walls*. Paternoster, 2002.
Jones, S. *Why Bother with Church?* InterVarsity Press, 2001.
Mission-Shaped Church (a brilliant report put out by Church House Publishing), 2004.
Tomlin, G. *The Provocative Church*. SPCK, 2002.

Chapter 3 "Christians are such hypocrites"

Hare, J. E. *Why Bother Being Good?* InterVarsity Press, 2002.
Keene, M. *Christianity*. Lion, 2002.
Lewis, C. S. *Mere Christianity*. Fount, 2002.

Chapter 4 "Religious people are too intolerant"

Nonhebel, C. *Don't Ask Me to Believe.* Lion, 1998.

Chapter 5 "You can't trust the Bible"

Bruce, F. F. *The New Testament Documents: Are They Reliable?* 1960. Revised ed., InterVarsity Press, 2003.
Burridge, R. *Four Gospels, One Jesus.* SPCK, 1994.

Chapter 6 "Science has disproved Christianity"

Dembski, William A. *The Design Revolution: Answering the Toughest Questions about Intelligent Design.* InterVarsity Press, 2004.
Jeeves, Malcolm A., and R. J. Berry. *Science, Life and Christian Belief.* Baker, 1998.
McGrath, Alister. *Dawkins' God: Genes, Memes, and the Meaning of Life.* Blackwell, 2005.
Polkinghorne, John. *Belief in God in an Age of Science.* Yale University Press, 2003.
Ratzsch, Del. *Science and Its Limits.* InterVarsity Press, 2000.

Chapter 7 "There's just too much suffering in the world"

Jones, J. *Why Do People Suffer?* Lion, 1993.
McGrath, Alister. *Why Does God Allow Suffering?* Hodder, 2000.
Meynell, M. *Cross-Examined.* InterVarsity Press, 2001.

Chapter 8 "All the religions in the world can't be true"

Goldsmith, M. *What about Other Faiths?* Hodder, 1999.

Green, Michael. *But Don't All Religions Lead to God?* Baker, 2002.

Chapter 9 "There's not enough proof for me to believe"

Sire, James W. *Why Should Anyone Believe Anything At All?* InterVarsity Press, 1994.

Wright, N. T. *Who Was Jesus?* SPCK, 1992.

Chapter 10 "Something two thousand years old can't be relevant today"

Anderson, J. *Evidence for the Resurrection.* InterVarsity Press, 1950.

Morison, Frank. *Who Moved the Stone?* 1930. Revised ed., Authentic Lifestyle, 1996.

Chapter 11 "If there is a God, why doesn't he send someone to help us?"

Green, M. *Who Is This Jesus?* Kingsway, 2004.

McGrath, Alister. *The Unknown God: Search for Spiritual Fulfillment.* Lion, 2002.

Chapter 12 "I'm still not sure I believe in God"

Carey, G. *The Great God Robbery.* Collins, 1989.

McGrath, Alister. *The Twilight of Atheism.* Doubleday, 2004.

Williams, P. *The Case for God.* Monarch, 1999.

Other Important Sources

Stott, J. R. W. *Basic Christianity.* InterVarsity Press, 1977.

Packer, J. I. *Knowing God.* Hodder, 1993.

Dr. Michael Green is an internationally respected evangelist and Bible teacher. He has written more than sixty books and is currently a senior research fellow at Wycliffe Hall, Oxford University, England. Formerly he was on the staff of Regent College in Vancouver, Canada. His biography has recently been published by HarperCollins.

Nick Spencer is a researcher and writer for London Institute of Contemporary Christianity and the Jubilee Centre.

Also available from **Michael Green**

"Science has defeated faith!"
"Jesus was just a good man."
"All religions lead to God."

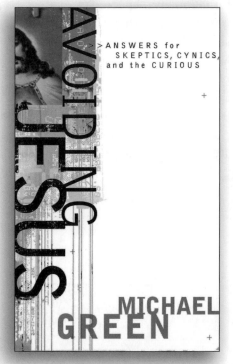

> ANSWERS for
> SKEPTICS, CYNICS,
> and the CURIOUS

People around the world offer these objections to Christianity every day. You've probably heard some of them. But have you truly considered all the possibilities?

Michael Green points out logical fallacies and often-overlooked evidence as he acknowledges valid questions and complaints about religion.

"With refreshing candor and careful reasoning, Michael Green answers the questions most often posed about the Christian faith. If you are a skeptic, cynic, or among the curious, you will find a friend in this book."

—**CHUCK COLSON**, founder, Prison Fellowship

More great tools for sharing your faith without fear

It could be the most important conversation you have with a loved one, and you don't want to risk pushing them away. Michael Green can help you navigate the potentially hazardous waters when sharing your faith with the ones closest to your heart.

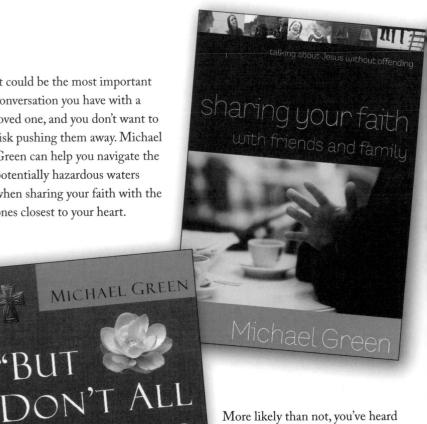

More likely than not, you've heard someone insist that sincere belief is what gets you to heaven, no matter what you put your faith in. Nothing could be further from the truth. Get the answers you need to help the religious pluralists in your life see the light.